Your First 90 Days in Network Marketing

How to Book Appointments and Make Money Fast in Your New Network Marketing Business

By Michael J. Durkin

To book MJ Durkin to speak at your next conference or sales meeting contact:

Prospectingcafe.com
Toll free: 1-866-350-6477
Outside the USA: 860-350-6477

Business and Speaking Tour Manager: Rick Franklin, e-mail:
rfranklin@prospectingcafe.com

Also by Michael J. Durkin

Double Your Contacts: *What Every Network Marketer Needs To Know About Making Contacts and Booking Appointments*

Double Your Downline: *Unlocking the Secrets to Network Marketing Success*

Selling from the Heart: *Weekly Visualizations, Inspiration and Strength for those that Sell*

Own Your Home Own Your Life!: *Beat the Bankers and Credit Card Companies at their Own Game, Pay Your Mortgage Off 15 Years Early and Retire Debt Free!*

To order go to: www.prospectingcafe.com

Your First 90 Days In Network Marketing

How to Book Appointments and Make Money Fast in Your New Network Marketing Business!

Michael J. Durkin

Published in New Milford, CT by *TruSource Publications, LLC*

Cover and book design by *Design Possibilities:*
Bonnie Skane, bonnie@prospectingcafe.com

Library of Congress Cataloging Publication Data

Durkin, Michael J., 1961 -

ISBN 978-0-578-04787-4

TruSource Publications, LLC, New Milford, CT

Contents

Speed is Your Friend -
Build it Fast and You'll Build it Big!

Head Trash vs. Belief -
Staying Strong When Making Calls

Your Most Valuable Asset -
Making Your Names List

Calling Close Family Members,
Friends and Neighbors

Approaching and Calling Organization Friends,
Neighbors and Casual Acquaintances

Approaching and Calling Close Friends
and Casual Acquaintances at Work

Dedication

To my sons, Tyler Michael and Corey Michael

Introduction

I am an outsider. I have never built a Network-Marketing business and so you might conclude that I do not have the experience or the wisdom to teach others how to build one. You may be right. However, my position as an observer allows me to be objective in a way that perhaps others cannot. I have no biases or loyalties to any one particular company, product or business building system. I get to see many of the finest companies, products and various methods of recruiting and retaining. Perhaps not being an expert on one company's methods makes me an authority on many – I'd like to think so.

I am an expert on one subject, however, and that is how to get in front of prospects. I spent twelve years of my business life selling at the kitchen table night after night, persuading couples to use my products and company over a plethora of tough, price cutting, competitors. I've had my share of canceled appointments, *"no shows"* and *"dark houses."* I recruited and trained straight commission salespeople, did millions of dollars worth of business each year and, at one point, had over 15 salespeople reporting directly to me. Our success was predicated on one salient point: in order to make the sale we had to first start with a name and a number (a lead) and we had to find a way to turn that name and number into an appointment. I believe that success in your business is predicated on that same critical issue. If you can turn a lead (a name and a number) into an appointment to tell the unique story of your product or service, YOU can build the kind of profitable business that your sponsor promised you the first time you saw your opportunity. This book is designed to help you put a name and number on a List and will show you how to get in front of that person to tell your story.

There are a number of things you should consider before you read this book:

1. **Listen to your sponsor, enroller, Vice-President or whomever brought you into the business.** Follow their system and trust them. This book is not meant to replace anything that they say to you or that they have taught you. It is simply designed to *"add to"* or fill in some of the gaps in the area of prospecting. You may need to *"read between the lines"* as you apply my material to your system. Insert these ideas into the places in your system where you may need a little clarification or an edge. Take what you like and leave the rest!

2. **This book is not the be-all and end-all to Network-Marketing.** It is for the brand new person that has just entered the industry. It assumes that you have a warm-market or at least a lukewarm market of prospects and that you have some measure of credibility with them. Inside these pages you will get tips on how to get a fast start in your new business with people that you already

know. It does not contain advanced techniques in how to put new people on your List after you have gone through your warm market.

3. **You must be willing to read this book at least 5 times!** If you won't do that, then you won't really be able to master this material. No one enters a black belt judo competition after two or three lessons or shows up to play at Carnegie Hall after practicing the piano for a couple of weeks. Relationship-Marketing is a career. Take it seriously. Learn your craft. Study it and get good at it. The concepts and verbiage that are included in this book, while not complicated will need to be studied and rehearsed. Drill for skill by practicing with your sponsor, your new distributors or your spouse.

4. **Get going and do it fast!** Here is a Network-Marketing riddle for you: Question: *"If you sponsor one person every month for 12 consecutive months, how many distributors or reps will you have in your downline?"* Answer: *"12?"* No, the answer is *"0"* because they will all be gone by then! Do not delay. Sit down with your sponsor. Make your List of names and punch the buttons on a phone and actually CALL THEM! NOW! Don't wait until you get the presentation down or know what you're doing. You'll never really be at the point where you really know what you are doing so CALL, CALL, CALL. You know more than

your prospect so CALL and get in front of them right away.

5. **You can re-restart your business at any time** – If you are not new to your business or the industry, you may not have jumpstarted your business fast in the first 90 days. You may have languished around with your opportunity for several years. That's okay. I suggest that you do not beat yourself up in any way for what you think you should have done but didn't. Feeling frustrated or getting down on yourself for not taking advantage of your company's products or opportunity is a sure fire way to cut off the flow of abundance. Bad feelings won't produce good income. However, you can use this book to *"restart"* your business. Perhaps you are ready (for whatever reason) to commit to taking massive action. This book can be the launching pad for you to give it everything you've got. I suggest that you do!

If you can keep these things in mind as you read this book and start to put the concepts that are discussed into action then this book will be worth the money you paid for it. If these techniques get you just one extra appointment or just one recruit that you might not have sponsored, it can make a huge difference in your business. However, if you are not really ready to commit to mastering this material or taking action, then you have actually just bought another *"shelf-help"* book. That's just another positive thinking book that will sit in your collection of books, CD's and training programs that you have never even read or listened to. I can't stand the idea that you invested money in this book and then won't use it. If you have just realized you are not ready to get into action, then please call my office in Connecticut and speak to my customer service people at 860-350-6477 and ask for your money back. They will give you an instant refund with no questions asked.

If you are ready to get into action however, then keep reading. You have entered an industry that has not even seen the real, rapid growth that it can ultimately achieve. The Network-Marketing (or as you will hear me refer to it as Relationship-Marketing) industry is getting ready to explode with success like never before. It is the most progressive, timely business model that I have ever seen. As the world economy shifts, I believe that a performance based economy will be developed and that the Relationship-Marketing industry is poised to take advantage of this new way of doing business. You have brilliantly (or accidentally) joined a sleeping giant of an industry whose time has come. It is my hope that this book will help you take advantage of it and that everything you envisioned the first time you saw the opportunity that you have aligned yourself with, will become yours!

MJ Durkin
November 2009

Chapter 1

Speed is Your Friend – Build it fast and you'll build it big!

To succeed in your new Relationship-Marketing business, you need to do one essential thing and do it quickly – make money! Making money is the one motivator that blows away all the *"you can do it"* platitudes, the *"never give up"* speeches, the self-help books and the positive thinking one liners. When you are making money in your new business, you are pumped! When money is coming in as a result of your efforts, it's easy to put more effort in! When the checks are rolling in nobody has to tell you to make another phone call or book another appointment. You are self-motivated!

Making Money – The Doubt Killer

Seeing a profit in your new business right away eliminates the biggest business killer – doubt! When you are making money, you believe. You believe in your company, your products and services and yourself! When you believe, you take action. Nothing can stop you. Seeing bonus checks and commission checks prove to you that this can work!

Building Fast is Fun

Making money fast in your Relationship-Marketing business is what this book is all about. Building your business slowly is painful – it hurts! Building fast is fun because you are making money and so are the people that you introduced to your opportunity. When they're making money, they're excited, motivated and don't need you to baby sit them! When they're not making money, you need to pull, push, prod and *"motivate"* them to do something. That's hard work! You signed up with the company of your choice so that you could build a business that provided you with a residual income for the rest of your life. You didn't sign up to drag people along with you. Building your Relationship-Marketing business should be fun!

So, let's make it fun right from the beginning by taking off fast and making money right away.

Momentum

Relationship-Marketing is a momentum-dependent business. The very nature of this type of marketing is that it is based on the duplication of your own efforts. **In order to achieve leverage of your time, effort and activity, you must get things moving in your business and get them**

moving rapidly. Starting a Relationship-Marketing business closely resembles what a pilot has to do to get a jet plane up to cruising altitude. If you were a passenger in that jet and your pilot was taking off down the runway only giving the plane 30% throttle, you would be very upset! Ambling down leisurely down the runway taking his time is clearly not the way to get that 150,000 pound hunk of metal up into the air. As a passenger you would be freaked out because, even though you're not an aerospace engineer, you understand that the pilot needs to give the plane 100% throttle in the first 30 seconds of take off or you are going to run out of runway and you are going to crash!

Figuratively, that's what happens to millions of Relationship-Marketers. They hit the end of the runway at 30% throttle and they crash or they never even get into the cockpit and fire up the engines. **In order to be successful, you have to understand that speed is your friend and that the first 90 days after you sign up with your company is the runway of your new business.** Ambling leisurely down the Relationship-Marketing runway, waiting to get your presentation down, becoming an expert about the products or surfing the company's website will not give you the momentum that you need to be successful in your new venture. Getting enough speed for take-off and then maintaining momentum for 90 days is a key to your success. Take the beginning of your business very seriously.

Unconscious Cloning

The members of your team or downline will duplicate exactly everything you think, say and do. The speed of the team is always the speed of the leader. Even your thoughts about the business will be duplicated by your people so be very careful about the way you think. The way that you join your company, how long you take to make that decision, how many prospects you put on your list, how many calls you make your first week, how you follow up with your prospects, how you attend training calls or events will all be duplicated by the people that you bring into your business. The people that you recruit or sponsor are consciously and subconsciously watching and imitating everything that you do as it relates to your business. Always ask yourself this question, *"Would I want the members of my team to be building their businesses like I am?"* Make sure that you act accordingly.

The Purest Form of Motivation

The people on your team will take massive action, if they are doing one thing – making money! The people on your team will quit or become inactive because of one thing – they're NOT making money. That's why it's so important to understand that momentum is synonymous with making money! The quicker your team members make money the more motivated they will be. You very rarely have to talk people into taking action or keep giving them motivational speeches about why they shouldn't give up and quit, if they are receiving bonus checks or commissions. The number one reason that Relationship-Marketers quit in the first 90 days of their new business is that they don't see a return for their efforts. While there are many fringe benefits of being involved in Relationship-Marketing: personal growth, meeting great people, learning a new industry, attending exciting and life changing events, developing a new social network, the glue that holds it all together is that each person is making the money that they need or want to make. Don't underestimate this fact. If momentum is synonymous with making money for you, then it is also essential for every person that you bring into your organization.

Tips for Getting off the Ground Fast

1. ***Get in front of your warm market (close friends, family, neighbors and work associates) right away!*** Don't delay. Sometimes new Relationship-Marketers will have a tendency to stall a bit because they want to *"learn everything about the products and the business first."* They think that they have to explain the business as well as their sponsor or the person who enrolled them. You should be working very closely with the person who brought you into the business and leaning on them heavily to make calls with you to set up your first appointments.

5

Don't make these first calls yourself! Have your sponsor do it for you and/or you make them with your sponsor sitting with you or on a three way call. Remember, you know a lot more than your prospect does. Don't procrastinate by deluding yourself that you need to become an expert about your products or your compensation plan. Set up a time with your sponsor and make some calls! Don't worry if you screw it up or a good friend of yours won't meet with you. That's the business you're in! Sometimes your close friends or family will be interested in learning more and sometimes they won't. A *"No"* doesn't mean that the business won't work; it just means that someone was not ready for an opportunity as good as yours. That's all it means.

2. ***Be positive about the people that you want to join you in your new business but don't become too invested in any one particular person.*** It is very common to be excited about having a person that you love, like a family member come into the business with you. However, I have seen new Relationship-Marketers devastated when the person that they *"just knew would join,"* wouldn't even sit down to look at the opportunity. I remember an experienced Relationship-Marketer telling me, *"I was so sure that my mother and my sister would want to build this business with me. It was so perfect for all of us and I was wounded when they were indifferent to the idea. Now, I make $4,000 a month part-time three years later and I still*

can't stand it that they don't see themselves doing the business with me. It really bugs me." It is okay to be positive about the people closest to you joining with you. If they don't join you, just don't attach too much meaning to it. They just were not ready – that's all.

3. ***Think of people that are ambitious, sharp and that you have credibility with but understand that you can't predict who will be interested.*** High level distributors in your business will tell you that they cannot predict ahead of time who will be successful in your business and who will not. If they can't predict who will be interested and successful, then you probably can't either. There are too many unknown factors that affect whether or not a person will even take the time to sit down with you and listen to your opportunity. **You can't say the wrong thing to the right person.** You could make the worst phone call invite in the history of Relationship-Marketing and if that person is ready, they will meet with you despite your horrible, unprofessional approach! Conversely, you could make a perfect, smooth, professional call and have the person rudely reject you in 15 seconds or less! You have to understand: it's not you; it's them! Don't build a story around why someone wouldn't meet with you. They just weren't open to new ideas and you can't predict which ones will and which ones won't!

4. ***Shoot for giving your prospect a full presentation with all the facts.*** You may be very tempted to casually mention to your family, close friends, work associates or neighbors that you are benefitting from some new products or that you have started a new business. I call these *"over the fence"* conversations. You might mention it on the phone or in person to gauge what their reaction might be. They may see you taking a new product, see it on your kitchen counter or see it at your desk and ask you about it. While these types of conversations with you sharing your experience can cause someone to be interested and want more information, they usually are incomplete. They tend to start an interesting dance between you and your friend (prospect). This dance looks like you trying to follow up by giving them more information but trying not to sell them or trying to get them into something. While this can work, it usually takes a long time for the prospect to come around to ask to purchase the product or learn more about your business opportunity. Also, they are not seeing the business in its totality this way, so there are things that they won't understand or even get to see because of this *"piece meal"* approach. While there are exceptions to this rule, in general, you will not have much success just *"talking to someone about the business"* on the phone, in the grocery store, at the water cooler or at the bowling alley by *"mentioning"* the business. Remember, *"Speed is your*

friend" when building your Relationship-Marketing business. The more momentum you create the better and telling stories to your friends and family is more of a *"dripping"* method and it is a very slow process. **The optimum way to present your product and opportunity is to set up an appointment where your prospect is prepared to listen to something that relates to making money or whatever benefits your products or services provide.**

Line Up With Your Decision

Congratulations on your decision to start a Relationship-Marketing business! You may very well be a genius! The economic landscape has never before been so fertile to grow the type of business model that you have chosen. All the statistics tell us that Relationship-Marketing companies grow during an economic downturn. Prospects that would have turned their noses up five years ago to a Relationship-Marketing business, all of a sudden, will listen due to the financial insecurity that they may feel. There has never been a better time to build the business that you have chosen to build!

Obviously, you have picked a company with a product line or service that you believe in. That's great. So, now it's time to get into action! Relationship-Marketing businesses are performance-based – you get paid if you perform or produce something. The action that it takes to get your business profitable lies in how fast you can tell your unique story to as many people as you can. That's what this book is all about.

Chapter 2

Head Trash vs. Belief – Staying strong when making calls

It is important to know exactly what you have gotten yourself into if you have started a Relationship-Marketing business. **You have entered an industry where your success will be largely dependent on your ability to reach out to large numbers of individuals and share your ideas and enthusiasm about your product, services and company.** The very nature of Relationship-Marketing will propel you to be very pro-active in engaging people in a conversation about what you believe about your products and company. There is no way around this fact: the business that you are involved in is a prospecting intensive business. There. I've said it and somebody needed to say it. You don't have to be a good salesperson, have the gift of gab or be a great presenter to successful in Relationship-Marketing. You don't! However, you do have to become a great prospector. You have to get good at one thing and that's getting your story in front of a lot of people! And you should get used to the idea that you're going to be doing it for as long as you are in your business.

Belief Systems of New Relationship-Marketers

A Belief System is simply a thought that you think over and over again until it becomes a part of what you believe. The reason that I call it a *"system"* is that once it is entrenched in your psyche, it will tend to direct or drive you in a very unconscious or *"automatic"* way. The Belief Systems that are a part of us will cause us to either take certain actions or will inhibit us from taking certain actions. Your Belief Systems or what you believe are an essential part of who you are and those beliefs can either support your ability to build your new Relationship-Marketing business or are non-supportive of your ability to build your business. Let's focus on belief systems you'll need to cultivate in order to build your new business quickly.

Recommending Things You Like

As a new Relationship-Marketer you obviously saw something about the products, the opportunity or the company that made you want to enroll and start building your business. At some level, you believe that your new business can help the people that you know in some way. As you are preparing to make your Names List, think about your attitude or belief system around recommending things that you like to your friends. When you see a movie you really enjoy, do you tell people about it? When you eat at a great restaurant, do you mention it or rave about it to your friends? When you enjoy the new pastor and his sermons at your church, do you talk about it with people that you like? When your favorite store is having a huge sale and you got some really great deals, do you shout it from the rooftops to your friends? Of course, many of us operate this way because it is very natural to recommend things that we enjoy to our friends, neighbors or work associates who might also enjoy or at least want to hear about them.

As a new Relationship-Marketer, it is of great value for you to realize that recommending your products or opportunity works the same way. If you like something, you tell people about it. If you believe something is good, helpful or a good deal, you mention it to people that you know. There is no pressure to recommend something that you enjoy. As you get ready to make your List, be light and easy about it. Think about the benefits you have received from your association so far with your company. Imagine that you are just going to recommend or share your experience with the people that you are going to put on the List. It's just like telling people that you saw a great movie! That's easy!

Stay True to Your Beliefs

It is very possible and quite common that you might initially call some people that you know very well – people that you care about. It is important to remember that you are calling them to make appointments to share with them something that made a difference for you or that you believe in. **YOU ARE NOT TAKING A SURVEY!** You are not trying to get their opinion about whether or not you have done the right thing by getting into the right business or industry. You have already made that decision! This is very similar to having a particular political or spiritual belief. If you were to reach out to someone to discuss your spiritual beliefs and they didn't agree with your point of view or even attacked it, would you abandon your religion or your church? Of course not! You might even dig your heels in deeper and defend vigorously what you believe to be true, wouldn't you? When you get ready to make your calls, why you believe what you believe about your products, the company and the opportunity. You are not looking to get your family or friend's viewpoint on the validity of the business. You already know that you have that viewpoint. Make the calls to book appointments – that's all!

When They Are Ready – They're Ready!

Some of the prospects that you will put on your List have been praying for and searching for an opportunity to make more money or have had a desire to move toward more health and wellness. As we described before, you can't predict who they are going to be, so you simply need to get the products and the business in front of them and let THEM decide. Don't worry about not having enough knowledge about the products or being able to present the opportunity properly or professionally. YOU KNOW MORE THAN THEY KNOW ABOUT IT SO GO AHEAD AND SET UP AN APPOINTMENT AND EXPLAIN WHAT YOU KNOW! You can't say the wrong thing to the right person. Those people that are looking and have the drive, will and desire to improve their health or their finances, will respond positively. Those who are not, will not. There's not that much that you can do about that. Know that your job is to get the products and opportunity in front of those people and let them decide.

Create a Story That Supports You

When events happen to us in life, we frequently attach some kind of meaning to them. We often tell ourselves a story that supports what that event means to us. For example: If you call your best friend up and ask them to look at your opportunity and they say, *"No"* that they won't even look at it, you start to attach a certain meaning to that, *"No."* Here are several *"meanings"* that you might be tempted to give to that response:

"Oh no, this business isn't going to work for me if I can't even get my best friend to look at it."

"Wow. I thought I had credibility with that person. Maybe I don't have as much credibility with my friends as I thought I had."

"This isn't going to be easy. This is going to take a lot of hard work and time. I don't have the time to put so much energy into this, so maybe it can't work."

"Maybe it's because of me that they wouldn't take a look at my opportunity. These kinds of things never work out for me. Everyone else seems to be able to be successful with these kinds of businesses but not me."

"My best friend won't even look at the business and join me, so how am I going to make it work with people that I don't even know that well? I wondered if I had the skills or guts to do this business and this proves that I can't. I'll never make a lot of money. I was crazy to think that I could be successful in a business like this. I'm such a loser!"

So, you can see the stories that can be created out of a simple, *"No."* You can also see how they can start to spin out of control and start to gather more and more negative meaning. Let's look at the converse and see the kinds of stories that can just as easily be created and that would be more supportive:

"My friend is obviously not open to new ideas or alternative ways to make money."

"Hmm, she's not interested in looking at something. I thought she'd be more open minded considering that I

know she needs and wants more money. This is going to be fun, sorting through my friends and finding out which ones are ready to build something with me."

"This must not be the right time in my friend's life for them to be looking for a great opportunity. They must not be ready to look at something as good as this."

"They must have some pre-conceived notions about this type of business. I wonder why they would sell themselves so short."

"That's too bad. I thought they'd be great at the business. I guess it's their loss!"

"I'm surprised that they wouldn't even take a look. I'm very excited to be building this new business and where I'm going with this. It's too bad that they won't be taking this exciting journey with me. I can do this and I'm going to do it."

This second set of stories has a much different tone than the first set of stories, doesn't it? There is great value in understanding that YOU are the one who attaches the meaning to the event of the *"No"* and that you can create any story about the response that a prospect gives you. **A prospect can never reject you, unless you give them the power to reject you through the story that you tell yourself.**

Successful People Understand Success

It is very common for people new to Relationship-Marketing to put prospects on their Names List that NEED the benefits of their new business. Because you personally know most of the first 100 people that you put on your List, you may be aware of their level of need. They may have an acute need for the benefits or your product or service and they may have a desperate need for more money. When building a names List, you sometimes gravitate toward people that are hurting, jobless, losing their home or are in financial trouble. It makes sense to offer your new business to people that are down and out, but quite often, you will be shocked at how resistant they are to the idea of making more money with ANY opportunity, not just yours. You have to understand that many of them end up in this troubled place because they are pushing against abundance, wealth and opportunity. People that come from a place of scarcity will often be suspicious or negative about your opportunity, even though they need it the most! Don't judge them.

Your best prospects to put on your Names List are people who are already in a place of abundance, who are already very successful. **Successful people understand success and they are often very willing to sit down and look at a new idea or innovative concept.** Do not be intimidated by people that make a lot of money – be excited to put them on your List. Look for people that *"want"* more success, money, time, wellness, health and happiness, not people that *"need"* it. **Don't waste a lot of time trying to convince people that are broke that they need your business.** Attract the people that are already successful and are looking for more ways to attract more success!

It is Easy to Offend People That Want to Be Offended

Sometimes people that you know very well will respond derisively toward your approach. Quite frankly, they can be quite mean and nasty. A Relationship-Marketer recently told me about meeting with a prospect who they casually knew from a business relationship. He used my prospecting approach to set up a meeting with the prospect without giving many details about the business. In the first five minutes of my client's presentation, the prospect rudely stopped him and sneered, *"Is THIS what you wanted to talk to me about?"* as he pointed to a product sample that my client had pulled out of his bag as if it were a dead animal. My client looked him in the eye and said, *"Yes, this is exactly what I came to talk to you about."* *"Well,"* the prospect huffed, *"This is not my thing. I certainly would not be interested in something like THAT,"* he said in a disgusted tone. My client stayed strong, again looking the prospect dead in the eyes and said, *"That's fine. I respect your feelings and I'm not one of those Relationship-Marketers who pushes things on people that don't want to hear about them"* and he put the sample back in his bag. True to his word, he changed the subject, asked the prospect some questions about himself, offered to help him in his business and then excused himself to go to his next appointment. Some people are looking for a way to be offended by anything and your approach about your new business is just one more reason for them to be negative about something. **Remember that you can't offend, bother or interrupt anyone – they allow themselves to be offended, bothered or interrupted.** If your intentions are good and positive, then stay strong about what you have to offer and don't let anyone's negatively cause you to doubt yourself for a second! Did your prospect offer you a way to make money or feel better physically? No, they had nothing to offer, so don't worry if they are offended that you wanted to help them and get paid for helping them. Bless them, allow them to be who they want to be and move on to the next prospect.

You Have to Make a Lot of Calls

You should be positive and expect to get an appointment every time you reach out and make a call. **However, as I described earlier, you have entered a prospecting intensive business and that part is never really going to go away no matter how successful you become.** The nature of prospecting is also somewhat one-sided because you can never control what is going to happen on the other side of the phone, when you are trying to fill your calendar with appointments. Leaving messages that don't get returned, prospects that say that they have no time to meet with you, prospects that have legitimate scheduling issues and last minute cancellations, are all a part of the prospecting business. You can't control what your prospects will do, so you will have to get used to that idea. You can, however, control one thing on your side of the fence: that is, how many times you call and put energy out there to invite people to experience your products and opportunity. In Relationship-Marketing you have to *"punch-buttons"* (because we don't dial anymore) on a phone a lot and you have to do it all the time! That's the business you got into!

Making Calls Should Be Fun

If you can line up with the fact that you have to make a lot of calls and talk to a lot of people to be successful in your new business, you might as well have some fun doing it. Punching buttons on a phone can be fun if you let it be fun. Here are some tips to make calling all the time a little lighter and easier:

1. *Be light and easy when you are making your calls.* The more relaxed you are the better. Don't worry about saying the wrong words or using the wrong approach – just let it fly! Even experienced Relationship-Marketers will tell you that they mess up their calls all the time! They just make more of them then other people. Remember, you can't say the wrong thing to a person who is ready, willing and open to looking at something. Conversely, you could deliver the exact lines off your script professionally and confidently

and be rudely dismissed by someone who is not ready, willing and open. That's on them – not on you!

2. ***Don't be too attached to a result when you start punching the buttons to make your call.*** There are a myriad of reasons why you might not get through or get the appointment that you want. If the only time you feel euphoric or excited is when you get an appointment then you are going to have trouble feeling successful. When you don't feel successful, you won't make calls. If you are making the calls and making them consistently allow yourself to feel successful because you are at least making them! If you make the number of calls you wanted to make for that day, even if you don't get the results you were hoping for, acknowledge yourself and be proud of it. You are doing the activity that you need to be successful in your new business. Always give yourself credit for making the calls, even if you didn't fill your calendar.

3. ***Enjoy your prospects!*** You'll find that they're a little crazy. Their excuses for not seeing you or not returning your calls can range from interesting to bizarre! You have to remember that your warm-market prospects are a little puzzled by your pro-active approach, all of a sudden and need to have coffee with them to talk about something. Cut them some slack and have a little fun with them. If you are easy about the call and meeting with them, then they will be too. If you are all uptight and businesslike on

them all of a sudden, they're going to freak and give you all kinds of resistance. Enjoy them, be relaxed about meeting with them and mess with them a little bit.

4. *In the recorded history of Relationship-Marketing (since 1959) no distributor, associate, consultant or rep has ever been physically killed because a prospect said "NO" to them.* No one has ever died from hearing the word *"No."* **A *"No"* is not about rejection unless you make it about rejection!** Why would you take a prospect's resistance to look at a new idea to make money personally? It has nothing to do with you! It has everything to do with them. Toughen up! Get a thicker skin! Don't be so dependent on what other people think of you. If they say *"No"* to meeting with you, I guarantee you that they will just go back to eating their pasta and won't even give you a second thought! So, why should you give them a second thought? A *"No"* has no meaning unless you give a meaning. I suggest you just ignore it.

5. *Allow yourself to grow.* In my book, *Selling from the Heart,* I say that selling is the most intense, fun, personal development program that I have ever enrolled in – and they paid me to take the course! Prospecting will cause you to grow. You'll learn a lot about yourself by making calls to book appointments. You will have a chance to see just how quick, fun and sharp you can be when making calls. **Each call that you make can be a creative**

adventure, if you let it be. Every time you have an interaction with a prospect, you can come out of it a little stronger, wiser more confident, if you allow yourself to learn from it.

What business are you in?

Hopefully you are clear now that you are in the prospecting business! If you accept this fact, then you can see how important it is for you to have your *"inner game"* (your belief-systems) strong as it relates to prospecting. Feeling good and confident about approaching people is the cornerstone to being successful in your new venture. It is essential that you get your head together on this subject. If you have beliefs that don't support your ability to put people on a List and make the calls, then get with your sponsor, enroller or whatever you call them in your business and ask for their help. Lean heavily on them for support in the beginning. Their beliefs about calling are strong, so let them carry some of the load as you launch your business. This is not to say that you shouldn't become self-sufficient and self-reliant. You should! Aspire to be able to get out on your own and make your own appointments as soon as you are ready. It is a skill that will feed you for a lifetime! Now, you can have your inner game strong but if you don't have anyone to call, it doesn't matter how confident you are. That's what the next chapter will focus on.

Chapter 3

Your Most Valuable Asset – Making your names list

The most powerful asset that you bring to your business is the List of people that you know. This is literally a List of everyone that you have ever met in your life. Some experts say that the average adult has met and *"knows"* over 2,000 people and could theoretically write those names down on a List. This might be a stretch for the most part but the fact is that you have come into contact with many people in the course of your life and you *"know"* them. We put quotations around the word know because there are many different levels of how you might know someone, which we will discuss in a minute. As you get ready to make your List of names, keep in mind the basic premise of Relationship-Marketing. Relationship-Marketing or as it is sometimes called, Network-Marketing, is effective because it is based on a person's willingness to leverage the relationship that they have with someone to explain or share a concept or a product with them. Trying to explain all of the benefits of your unique products would be very difficult with traditional advertising, like television, commercials or magazine ads. Your company's products and opportunity have such a unique story that the story is best told person to person. Only then can the products and their benefits be fully explained and explained by someone who is credible and believable – you!

The Initial List is Not Your Only List

This initial List of Names is just one of many that you will be making in your career in Relationship-Marketing. It is not the be-all and end-all of Lists. It is your initial List to jumpstart your new business. Remember, the key to a Network-Marketing business is leveraging the relationships that you have in order to tell the unique story about your experience with your products and the company. As you mature and grow in your association with your business, you will meet new people, join new groups and expand your circle of relationships. You will be constantly adding names to the List and continually presenting the products and opportunity to more people as you go on. This part, the meeting of new people and presenting will allow your business to continue to expand in the future. If your List is small right now, don't worry about it – I'll show you how to expand it. If your List is large right now – that's great; I'll show you how to move fast and show your opportunity to everyone on the List so that you can get all the names off the List.

A Big List Equals a Big Business

Put everyone that you know on the List for now. Just brainstorm names. Write down every name that you can think of. Don't worry if they live far away or you think that they won't be interested. Just put every name on the List for now. You can choose not to call someone for any reason if you wish, but for now just get as many names on paper as you can.

Categories of Names

There is a reason that you want to break your Names List into categories. This is because the call to each category is different depending on your relationship with that person. Remember, since Relationship-Marketing is based on leveraging the relationship between two people, it is of value to categorize your relationship with each person on your Names List. The premise here is that the kind of call you would make to a family member or close friend is different from the call you would make to a stranger that you just met the other day in a coffee shop. Before you read the next section, go to www.prospectingcafe.com to download and print a blank copy of the *"List."* When you have the List next to you and a pen or marker in your hand, start reading the next section and every time that you think of a name in a category, write it down on the List. Don't worry about the phone numbers or how to contact each person right now. If the number is handy write it in the space provided. Just write down as many names as you can, as you think of them. Your goal is to write down 100 names on a List as quickly as you can. The following illustration gives you the categories. I call it the *"Circle of Trust."* The people closest to the center trust you the most. The people at the furthest rim from the center do not trust you as much. It is of great value for you to understand that the way that you will approach people close to the center is much different from the way you will approach those at the furthest reaches of the center.

The Circle of Trust

Family Members

This includes your immediate family, like your mother, father, sisters and brothers. It could also include any relatives that you are close to like aunts, uncles or cousins. The key here is that you have a fairly close relationship with them, see them frequently or spend a lot of time with them. A long lost cousin that you haven't seen or talked to in ten years doesn't really belong in this category. Family that you love deeply and that you are very close to goes on this List.

Close Friends

These are people that you see or talk to a lot. You have a close relationship with them and are in contact with them often. These are the kinds of friends that you could call in the middle of the night to come and get you if your car broke down or you needed them to watch your kids if you had to run out at a moment's notice. These are not long lost college friends or a friend from work from ten years ago. These are friends other than family that you would invite to a party, barbecue or celebration, like a christening, birthday party or graduation party. They are people that you consider to be close to you -people that you truly care about.

Neighbors

These could be people that live on either side of your home or anyone that you know due to where you live. These neighbors usually fall into the close friend category or the casual acquaintance category. They can also be neighbors that you have not spoken to in a long time and they could come under the category of long lost acquaintances.

Organization Friends and Casual Acquaintances

These are people that you know through the different organizations you belong to. You may like them and you may be friendly with them but they are more acquaintances than people you would invite to a christening for your new baby or a family oriented social function at your house. Read each organization and stop to write some names on your List as you think of the people that you know as a result of being a part of these groups or activities. For example: by attending your child's baseball games, you may know many adults there because you attend and cheer the kids on. Other groups would include: Church, Committees at Church, Volunteer Work, Adult sports teams (bowling, softball, basketball etc.), Gym, PTA, Kids' School Related Committees, Your Kids' Sports Teams, Yoga class, Mission work, Play group, Nursery School, Crafts classes, Lions club, Rotary, Chamber of Commerce, Networking Groups, Political clubs, etc.

Included in this category are people that you know casually. It could be other parents at the bus stop or people that you just bump into and know but are not really close to. You may know their names but you probably don't know much about them and they probably don't know much about you. You know them enough to smile at them and say hi. In this category of people, you probably don't even have their contact information such as their cell number.

Close Work Friends and Casual Work Acquaintances

These are people in your workplace that work for you or you work for them. This includes your boss, your co-workers or your subordinates. Don't worry at this point about whether you want them to know about your new business or if it is even ethical to talk with them at this point. Just put every person you know at work down on the List. We will talk more about contacting them in the section on actually calling them.

Work Related Casual Acquaintances

These are people that are around the periphery of your work related life. These could be vendors that call on you, suppliers, customers, service people who come into your building like delivery people or the copy repair person. They can be anyone that you come into contact with as a result of doing your day to day work. Imagine your work day, think of every one that you come into contact with and write them in this category.

Long Lost Friends and Relatives

These are people that you *"know"* but you have not talked to in a while. You may have been very close to them at one time but you may have drifted apart or moved and your life is much different from theirs now. These are still great people to put on your List, even if you are getting their names from your high school yearbook or they live a long distance from you.

Long Lost Casual Acquaintances

These are people that you casually knew but have lost touch with. This is usually someone that you knew at work or a church you used to go to and they pop into your head as someone who you think would be very interested or very good at doing your type of business. You might think to yourself that they are not a good prospect because you didn't know them well in the first place and it's been years since you've talked to them. Put them on your List anyway. Remember you are just brainstorming as many names as you can get on the List for right now – and I'll show you how to make that call in the next section. It's easy but it has to be approached the right way.

People You Buy From Outside of Your Home

This includes every person that provides some kind of service or product that you need to operate your life. In most cases, you know these people as acquaintances but you may see some of them on a daily basis and be fairly friendly with them. Let's imagine that you leave you house in the morning. What does your daily routine look like? Picture all the places that you stop on the way to work or on the way home from work. Fill in the following sentence and think of the people that you meet at these places – Places you buy _____ from: Gas, coffee, breakfast, groceries, convenience items, lunch, clothes, household items, dry cleaning, postage, shipping, flowers, parking, newspapers, magazines, DVD's, CD's, automotive, party goods, books, cell phones, computers and accessories, copying, travel, dental, dog grooming, spa services (nails, facials, etc.), insurance, financial services, carpets, flooring, hardware, gifts, fitness, chiropractic, hearing aids, pool supplies etc. You can see that the list can go on and on. Many of us, in the course of our daily lives, come into contact with many people. Sometimes on a repeat basis and sometimes it's just a one-time shot. In the course of your day, running errands, picking kids up, going to doctor's appointments and stopping in at various stores to pick up cough syrup, a new blender or a pack of gum you meet people! Start noticing those people and start thinking of them as people that are interested in more wellness and more money. For now, just write down the ones that you see on a repeat basis and know by face or by name. You might even have to write down, *"Guy behind the deli counter who gives me my bagel every morning"* because you don't know his name yet. That's okay. By writing that description down, it becomes more likely that you will end up introducing yourself to him and have a chance to get his number.

People That You Buy From for Your Home

This is a category unto itself because you invite many people into your home to sell you things that you need for your home. You also have service and delivery people show up at your house – some of them on a fairly regular basis and some come to handle certain projects. Delivery people like UPS, FEDEX and your Post person are just some *"regulars"* that come to mind. Monthly service people like pest control, lawn care, oil and gas delivery and meter people are also great prospects. At the very least, you smile and say hi to most of them when they come to your home. At the very most, you may know their names and have a friendly relationship with them. Put them on the List. You may have some of the following professionals come to your house for various reasons. Write the names down as you read this: Electrician, Carpenter, Painter, Lawn care, Arborist, Flooring, Decorator, Paving, Basement Waterproofing, Water Conditioning, Window Treatments, Cable Television, Newspaper delivery, House Cleaning, Kitchen and Bath Remodeling, Oil Delivery, Heating and Air Conditioning, Building Contractor, Alarm

Systems, Caterer, Excavator, Landscaping, Plumber, Realtor, Fencing, Windows, Wells and Pumps and so on.

New People That You Will Meet

From this moment on, EVERYONE that you come into contact with is a potential prospect for your products and opportunity. This means EVERYONE. When you are out and about in your daily life, anyone *"new"* that you meet that is not in one of the previous categories of someone that you *"know"* is someone that you want to meet, get their name and number and put it on your List. It is of great value for you to start thinking about meeting new people with the intention of getting their contact information. **Even if you made a List of 500 people that you know – eventually that List is going to run out. If you are adding new names from this moment on, then you will never run out – that's one of the keys of going to your first promotion level and beyond!** Since this book focuses on the new Relationship-Marketer and the use of your warm-market, we will not spend any major time discussing how to contact new people and adding them to your List. In my book *Double Your Contacts: What Every Network-Marketer Needs to Know About Making Contacts and Booking Appointments,* I discuss this process in great detail for the Relationship-Marketer. You can find that book at www.prospectingcafe.com.

More Places to Find Names

You have many sources of Lists of names that you can look at that can jump-start your memory. Here a just a few: Address book in your cell phone, address book in your email list, mailing list in a data base like Act or Goldmine, high-school or college yearbook, Christmas card mailing list, sports rosters (your teams and your kids' teams), Facebook or My Space pages etc. Look through the pictures that you have saved on your phone, on Facebook or in your computer. Remember, each time you see something that jogs your memory about a person, write their name down immediately. Don't try to judge anything about whether they would be interested or not, be good at the business or not or you would feel comfortable approaching them. Just write their name on the List.

Carry the List Around With You

As you go about your day, keep your List with you. Have it on your person, in your briefcase, next to your computer at work or on the kitchen counter as you are making dinner. As you are doing your daily activities, names will pop into your head of people that should be on your List. As you think of them and since the List is with you, you can easily write them down on the List and capture them on paper before they fly out of your head.

Getting Ready to Approach Your Names List

Once you have 100 names, go back over the List and fill in phone numbers as much you can by looking in your cell phone address book, calling directory information, writing down the phone number of the business that they work for and so on. Don't worry if you don't have a phone number for them right now. Just having the name on the List is stating your intention to contact that person. You may be surprised how the number shows up or even the exact person shows up in your experience. Now that have a working List with as many names on it as you can put on it, you are ready to start making some calls to book appointments. The next chapter will give the exact words that you can say to get the appointment.

Chapter 4

Calling Close Family Members, Friends and Neighbors

The Direct Approach

Now that you have your List of 100 plus names, it is time to get down to business – and have some fun! The fun is calling the people on the List to set up a time when you can show them a business and some products that made a difference for you. The way to be successful in your new business is to get the products and opportunity in front of as many people on your List as quickly as you can. You do this by setting up an official appointment to meet with them in some way to give them an ENTIRE PRESENTATION! This is not as hard as it may seem and actually should be done very simply. This conversation can be as short as 10 minutes. You will know that they are engaged in the direct approach when it has these elements included:

1. You have the prospect's name and phone number on a List.

2. You call the prospect, tell them you want to meet with them to explain something to them (more on that later).

3. You set up an official appointment to explain something to them. This can take many forms, from inviting them to attend an opportunity meeting to meeting them for coffee to discuss something.

4. You actually meet with them in person (or whatever version of your first step is recommended by your sponsor) to explain how or why you enrolled as a distributor with your company (you tell your personal story). Then you explain the concepts or philosophy of your company (tell the company story) and you explain how the products or services can help them. Then you explain your compensation plan and how they can make money by taking the products, using your services or by building a business. You then ask them if they would like to buy the products or enroll as an associate!

Now, you have actually *"talked to someone about the business"* the proper way. They have all the information to make an informed decision. Hopefully their decision will be to jump in, enroll, buy your initial starter pack, make a list of names and get you in front of a bunch of their friends right away! If they are ready to make that decision and move quickly, you haven't lost any time in slowly *"dripping"* on them to get them convinced. They can start making money right away and you can start making money right away. And remember, the number one reason that people drop out of Relationship-Marketing is that they aren't making money fast enough. This approach allows the person that has the drive or the desire to take their new business and run with it fast! **Speed is your friend in your new business. Never forget that.**

If your prospect is not ready to make that decision, then NOW is the time to start *"dripping"* on them or following up. Giving them literature, DVDs, product samples and telling them stories over a period of time CAN work. We will talk about how to set up a follow up appointment later on.

Calling to Set-Up Appointments

If it is possible, set up an evening or time when your sponsor can be there to help you make your first calls. They can sit right there with you, or if it makes you nervous, they can sit in the other room. With your sponsor there, you can get tips and hints from them and they can even jump on the phone with your prospect and help you to get the appointment. Don't do these first calls by yourself if you can help it. If your sponsor lives far away, perhaps you can conference them in on each call, so that they can hear everything for coaching purposes and they can jump in to help if needed. For purposes of this discussion about calling, we will assume that your sponsor is nearby but that you are handling the actual calling by yourself.

Review Your Belief Systems Before Calling

What is a belief system? A belief is a thought that you think over and over again until it becomes truth to you. It is real to you and it will cause you to react automatically to certain statements or responses. Let's review the supportive belief systems that we already discussed and give you a few new beliefs that will support your ability to make the calls:

1. **It is normal and right to recommend things that you like or enjoy, like a good movie or a good restaurant.** You are calling your close friends, relatives and neighbors to recommend something that you feel is a good deal and they should know about. Whether they choose to take advantage of your recommendation is up to them, not up to you. All you can do is make the offer.

2. **There is no way that you can pre-determine who will be interested in your products, services or opportunity.** You do not have psychic powers and you don't know ahead of time what part of the business might appeal to someone. Only when you have met with them in person and shown them the beginning, the middle and the end of the presentation, will you know for sure. That's why your only goal when calling is to get them to meet with you to simply listen.

3. **You are not taking a survey.** You already believe in your company, products and opportunity. Many of the people

that you call may have opinions about the industry or your involvement with your particular company. And that's what they are – opinions! People have all sorts of opinions about what is right for them but it does not mean that their opinion is right for you. If your company has made a difference for you in your life, stay strong in what you believe. Don't allow others to manipulate your beliefs.

4. **When people are ready, they are ready!** Your ability to explain the benefits of your products, services or opportunity is just not that important. When someone has drive and desire and the timing is right for them, just presenting them with a decent idea is enough – they will see the potential and want to get involved. If someone is not ready, you could be a master salesperson and closer and you won't be able to get them interested. Again, that's why it's so important to realize when you are making your first calls, that you just need to get the chance to give them a full presentation – then THEY can decide what is right for them and what is not.

5. **You do not have to have any one particular person come into the business for the business to work for you.** It is very common to think of people that you think would be great for the business and you should be positive about them joining you. However, the danger here is that some of the people that you think would be great will not even sit down and meet with you. This may be due to

timing or due to their own biases. We know that it would be great if your closest family or friends came along with you on this journey, but you don't need THEM to be successful in the business or to validate your decision. The good news is that people that you would never think would be interested or even good at doing the business, WILL join you because the timing is right and they are ready! These people will become your first leaders in your business and you'll be glad you decided to show them a full presentation.

Making the Calls – Calling Close Family Members, Friends and Neighbors

Remember that the people that are in this category are people that you are close to. They are people that you would invite into your home. They are people that you respect and love. As such, they are a very interesting category of prospects. On one hand, you have the ability to talk with them like very few people can. You have access to them. You have their phone numbers, know when you can reach them and know they will return your call if you leave them a message. Theoretically, they trust you. These are people that, if you said to them that a movie was good or that a restaurant was bad, would take you at your word and would value your opinion. On the other hand, the minute that you start to ask them to listen to a business idea that you are going to profit from, the dynamic sometimes changes. On your side, you believe they would be good in the business, you'd like them to build it with you (you might be convinced that they are going to love what you show them and will jump at a chance to join you) and you may also know that they need the benefits of your products or your compensation plan. You also expect them to trust that your judgment is sound. On their side, they sometimes can be a little surprised that you are suddenly making a recommendation about something with such excitement or need for them to believe you. Sometimes they feel the dynamic change because they sense that you want them to be convinced – that you need something from them. This can cause them to have resistance and can even prevent them from wanting to even listen.

So the fact that you know them so well and see them all the time is somewhat of a blessing and something of a disadvantage. The good news is that you can probably leverage the relationship that you have with them to get them to listen to an idea and take the time to listen to it because it is YOU who is asking them. The bad news is that if they feel that you are moving into *"selling"* or trying to push them into something because you are going to get something out of it, their resistance can go up. Sometimes your friends and family are especially concerned about looking at something that you want to *"present"* to them because they feel very uncomfortable having to say, *"No"* to you if they want to say, *"No."*

When you are showing your opportunity to close friends and relatives, you want to use a fairly subtle and laid back approach. The good news about your family and close friends is that once you have shown them the business, you do have the ability to *"drip"* on them after you show them the details of your business. You can give them samples and you can tell them stories about how the products are making a positive change in your life and they can see by your example that you are healthier, happier, more positive and making extra money!

Script # 1

Calling a Close Family Member, Friend or Neighbor

Son: *"Hi Mom, how are you?"*

Mom: *"I'm good. How are you?"*

Son: *"I'm good Mom. Mom, do you remember my friend, John? Well, John met some very successful people from _____ (mention a city, state or country where your sponsor or upline is from) who are building a fast growing business and they are expanding. I think the idea has some great potential. As a personal favor to me, I just need you to listen for a few minutes about the concept because I want you to know what I'm thinking of doing and there might be some money making* *potential for you. What night should I come over for coffee? Is Monday good or is Tuesday night better?"*

Mom: *"Well sure honey, but what's it all about? Can't you tell me about it over the phone?"*

Son: *"Mom, I'd rather not get into the details on the phone. It's better if I just talk to you in person. It will make more sense for both of us. Is that okay?"*

Mom: *"Sure, I guess so."*

Son: *"Good. When should I come over? Monday night or Tuesday night?"*

Mom: *"Well Tuesday is good but I don't understand what all the secrecy is about. Why can't you tell me about it right now and give me some idea of what it's about?"*

Son: *"Mom, you trust me, don't you?"*

Mom: *"Sure son, I trust you."*

Son: *"I thought so. Do me this favor, would you? I just need you to listen for 15 minutes; that's all. Can you do that for me?"*

Mom: *"Sure son, we can do that for you. Come over on Tuesday night. I'll bake a cake."*

Nuances of the Script

You can see here that you are leveraging the relationship to get your family member or close friend just to listen. Remember, just because they will listen or watch a presentation does not mean that they are interested, ready to make some changes or are even open minded. Notice some key phrases in the previous script:

1. *"As a personal favor to me"*

2. *"It's better if I just talk to you in person – it will make more sense for me and for you. Is that okay?"*

3. *"You trust me, don't you?"*

4. *"Do me this favor, would you?"*

Again, it is important to realize that you just want them to listen for a bit. You are trying to avoid having to give them any details before you can give them a full presentation. The minute you start giving details, you can start to get into trouble. If you mention the benefits of your products, service or Relationship-Marketing, they may start to make a pre-judgement about what it is and may never sit down to listen to you. Sometimes new Relationship-Marketers get very hung up on the fact that their closest family or friends would not even show up at an opportunity night or wouldn't have coffee to discuss the concept in complete detail. We can assure you that this is very common and if it happens, don't let it wound you! Just because the people that you love won't sit down and listen, does not mean that you don't have a viable, exciting business that you can build. It just means that they won't listen – that's all!

Too Many Details Can Kill Your Appointment Making

By the way, I suggest that you lead with a more generic approach rather than giving details. Often, giving details over the phone results in activating some pre-judgement or bias that your family member or close friend may have. If their bias gets activated, they may NEVER be willing to even sit down and listen and that's NOT good for them or for you! **I am, however, NOT advocating lying, skirting the truth or not answering direct questions.** I'll discuss this is greater detail in chapter 7. This approach assumes that you can leverage the relationship that you have with this person that is close to you and that trusts you enough to sit down and listen to something. If your friend or family member asks you directly what it is, what the name of the company is or what kind of marketing model you want to talk to them about, I suggest that you answer them directly. Again, I would not go into tremendous detail and I would push to get the appointment so that you can explain everything to them because that IS the best thing for you and for them. Now, let's get back to calling.

If Your Prospect Already Knows What Business You Are Involved In

Here is another approach that you can use, especially if your close family member or friend already knows that you are building a Relationship-Marketing business. "**RM**" in these scripts stands for Relationship-Marketer meaning YOU!

Script # 2

Calling a Close Family Member or Friend Who Knows You Are In A Relationship-Marketing Business

RM: *"Hi John, its Susan. How are you? Good. Listen John, I know that you never met my friend, Bob, from _____. Bob and some very successful business people there put together a company that is growing fast and they are expanding into our area. I think the idea has some great potential. I want to sit down with you for twenty minutes and have coffee you and show it to you so you'll know what I'm doing. I think there is also some income potential there for you too. When could we get together? Would some morning for coffee be good or should we meet at Starbucks after work some night?"*

John: *"Well sure Susan, I'd love to meet you for coffee and talk. But is this about that supplement business that your Mom told me you got into?"*

RM: "Yes it is."

John: *"Well, I really don't believe in businesses like that. I've seen these multi-level things come and go. It's only the people that get involved in the beginning and are at the top of the pyramid that make any money."*

RM: *"John, I'm sure that is true. But I'm personally very excited about the potential of this concept and I want to just lean on you for a favor – I need your help. I need some practice learning how to present this concept and I want you to know what I'm doing just because you're my friend. If you would just indulge me and let me show you what I'm doing, when I finish I promise that if you don't see anything that interests you, I will never mention it to you again – I promise. Will you do me this favor and just listen to me – just this once?"*

John: *"Listen, I just don't want to waste my time and I don't want to waste yours either. I know ahead of time that I won't be interested."*

RM: *"Look John, I hear you loud and clear. My purpose is not to get you into the business with me, although honestly I would love it if you saw the same potential that I did and we could work together. I just know that if I don't get the chance to show you, it's always going to bug me that I didn't. If I show it to you and you say, "No," then I can move on and not have to worry about whether or not I've shown you the business. Besides, we've always been good friends and I want you to know what*

I'm doing, first, because it's something that I'm interested in and second, you might know some people you could refer me to. Would you at least listen for twenty minutes and have coffee with your old buddy, Susan?"

John: *"Well okay, but I'm just doing this to help you – I'm not interested."*

RM: *"And I appreciate it. What day do you want to meet? Is Tuesday good?"*

Note: If you have to leverage the relationship so heavily as in the last example, you should know that you don't have a very open minded prospect. Be light and easy about your approach to this prospect. Be willing to practice your presentation and maybe get some referrals from this person. Perhaps, serendipitously, they will be interested in the business on a personal level.

More Tips on Approaching Family and Close Friends

It is important that you don't try to explain too much *"over the fence"* to close friends and family before you sit down to explain anything to them. Try to get the entire presentation in front of them in one shot because it may be your only shot – for a while at least! Don't be afraid to leverage the relationship that you have with them to get them to just listen to a presentation. Don't listen to any of their excuses about why they don't want to listen! As friends, they owe it to you to at least listen. If they are close to you, you should be able to show up on their doorstep, ring the bell and when they come to the door, say: *"Hi. I have something I want to run by you. Can you put some coffee on so we can talk?"* You CAN be that direct. I will give you more tips in the presentation section about the nuances of presenting and following up with family and friends in a subsequent session.

Staying Out of Voice Mail Hell

It is inevitable that when you call some of your close friends, family and neighbors you will not be able to reach them, *"live."* There are two ways that you can proceed from here. The first two or three times that you call them, I would suggest that you just hang up and NOT leave a voice mail. Since you know them intimately, they should, as a general rule, see your name on their Caller ID and pick up! However, in this day and age, it is very probable that you will encounter even your closest friend's voice mail. Try to reach them live to deliver versions of the scripts that you have just learned. If you have called three or four times and have not reached them live, DO NOT leave a voice mail that is a version of an *"over the fence"* conversation. **Do not try to describe even to your closest friends, that you want to speak to them about a business opportunity of some sort.**

Simple is Better With Voice Mail

If you feel that you are wasting time by trying to reach someone *"live"* and you want to leave a message, keep it simple. The key to getting your close friends to call you back is to leave a message that is unencumbered and creates a little curiosity. When you get their voice mail simply say, *"Hi, Mom, it's Jake. Mom, give me a call when you have a chance. I've got a question for you."* That's it! Don't say: *"Hey, how are you doing" stuff* or anything like that. Just say, *"I've got a question for you. Call me,"* and leave your number if you feel that you have to. Thousands of my clients have learned this approach in my books and trainings. They report back that it is the easiest way to get people to return your call. Trying to leave details about your new business or saying that you *"have a business proposition"* to talk with them about will almost guarantee a delay in them returning your call.

Let's go on now to calling prospects that are a little further out from the center of the circle of trust – people that you don't know as well as your family.

Chapter 5

Approaching and Calling Organization Friends, Neighbors and Casual Acquaintances

There is a huge category of prospects in the people that you come into contact with as a result of the various clubs, organizations, committees and teams that you belong to. They can also be neighbors or in general, just casual acquaintances. These are people that you *"know"* but are not close with them at all. They are people that are a little further out from the center of the circle of trust. As we described before, you know them enough to say, *"Hi"* to them but not much more than that. If you have their cell phone number on a list somewhere, they might be a little surprised if, all of a sudden, they received a call from you. Chances are that you don't even have their cell number and will have to ask for it. So you can see that this approach to this category of people is quite a bit different from approaching the people that are very close to the center of the circle of trust.

Because you really don't know them, it would seem somewhat out of place for you to, all of a sudden, stop them and ask them for their cell number. So, guess what? You've got to get to know them. You might want to start warming them up for several weeks or even a month before you approach them. Find a way to stop them and talk with them a little. Something as simple as *"Hey Jen, you know I say hi to you all the time here but I don't know much about you. What do you do besides being Cody's Mom?"* This can start more of a relationship with the person. Once you have established a little more of a relationship, you can now use the technique of asking for their cell number in order to call them about something business related that you want to speak with them about

Script # 3

Getting the phone number of an Organization Friend or Casual Acquaintance

RM: *"By the way Jen, you probably don't know this about me but I have a business interest with some friends outside of being a lawyer. They have a business that's growing fast and even though the economy is down, they're expanding. They've asked me to make some introductions for them to people that I know that have drive, ambition and want to make more money. Does that sound like you?"*

Acquaintance: *"Well, sure but what is it all about exactly. What kind of business is it?"*

RM: *"They've figured out how to tap into the 100 million baby boomers in this country that want to look and feel better with a proprietary technology that they have developed. Now's not the time to go into the details, but if you give me your cell phone number, I can give you a call sometime and we can set up a time to talk when I can really explain things the right way. Why don't you write your cell number down on the back of this card? (RM handing them the back of a business card and a pen) I'll call you when I can."*

Acquaintance: As they are writing down the number, *"Can you tell me a little bit about the product or what the company does?"*

RM: *"It'll make more sense and it's better for both of us if we wait for a time when we can really talk and I can answer all of your questions. (RM looking at their watch) "We'll I've got to take off now. I'll call you when I can."*

Asking for names and numbers of people that you casually know is an essential step to setting up the call. You'll notice in this approach that there is no *"over the fence"* conversation trying to get the person interested in your product or opportunity. When asking for a casual acquaintance's cell number, it is usually best to ask for it when you are on the run or you are ending the interaction with the person. For example: If you are sitting next to your prospect at your kids' soccer game, you want to make the approach just as the game is ending and you are getting ready to leave the bleachers. You DON'T want to start the approach to get the number at the beginning of a 2 hour game so that they can sit there bombarding you with questions for two hours!

Script # 4

Calling an Organization Friend, Casual Acquaintance or Neighbor After You Get Their Phone Number

RM: *"Hi Jen, This is Charlene. Jen, do you remember the other day when I told you that I knew some very successful people that had a business that they were expanding? Good. Well, Jen, the reason for my call is to set up a time when you and I can meet for coffee for a half hour or so and I show how the company is expanding, what we're looking for and how we might work together. However, if I showed you something that didn't fit or make sense for you, would you be comfortable giving me your honest opinion and telling me it wasn't a good fit? Could you tell me, "No?"*

Acquaintance: *"Sure I can tell you "No."*

RM: *"Good. Now, I'm looking at my calendar. Would after work sometime be good or could we meet during a break during the day or at lunch?"*

Acquaintance: *"I guess we could meet sometime for lunch..."*

When you are calling people that you are not intimate with and close to you, can see that the approach is a little more technical, more businesslike. This is okay because you don't have the *"trust"* factor going for you like you do when you are approaching people that are close to you. Let's move on to another category of names that can potentially help fill your list – people you know from work.

Chapter 6

Approaching and Calling Close Friends and Casual Acquaintances at Work

There are many questions that may come up for you as you think about people that you work with and whether or not you should approach them about your business. Will your boss or company owner be upset with you if they knew about your new business? Would they frown upon you talking to their employees about a business opportunity? Will your subordinates look at you differently knowing that you have another business? Would mentioning your new business be disadvantageous to you in your work situation? Only you can answer these questions and you should consider them carefully. There are some ways to approach people that can minimize these issues which we will discuss in the next section. If you feel that approaching people at work would be damaging to your career, there are three things I would suggest that you look at:

1. You know many other people outside of work. Don't base building your business just on your work friends.

2. If you are unsure about how it might affect you at work hold off on approaching those people for now until you get some more experience in the business.

3. Make sure that your hesitancy about approaching your work friends is NOT an excuse not to have to approach people or an excuse not to build your business.

General Tips About Approaching People at Work

The work place is one of the most common areas where *"over the cubicle"* conversations happen. Avoid floating stories or anecdotes about your new business to see how people will react. Don't give verbal presentations about the business standing around the water cooler or at the lunch table. Avoid drawing your compensation plan out on a napkin for co-workers at break time. Remember that every prospect needs to see a full presentation from start to finish so that they can have all the information and make an informed decision. Here are some tips to help you approach work friends:

1. **Make the approach to get the person's cell number so that you can call them about something that you would like to discuss with them outside of work.** This method allows you to take your presentation away from the work place and gives you more control over the actual presentation of the information.

2. **Being at work gives you a built-in reason NOT to answer questions about the business or the subject that you want to talk with them about.** Giving incomplete information and then being turned down for any further discussion because your prospect *"knows they won't be interested"* is frustrating and isn't effective. If someone asks you to tell them about it now, you can politely say, *"I'd rather not discuss this while we're at work. It's better for you and for me if we talk about it outside of work."*

3. **Getting a phone number and an agreement from your work friend to take your call outside of work makes the whole approach more professional.** If you want to be taken seriously as a business person, it makes more sense to get the number so that you can call later to set up an appointment just like any business person would do. Donald Trump doesn't pitch ideas on the back of the golf cart! If he wants to meet with someone he sets up an appointment.

Calling Work Friends and Acquaintances

There are basically five types of categories of people that you can approach at work. They look like this:

1. **Close friends** – You would invite them into your home for dinner or a family event.

2. **Subordinates** – People that work for you or report to you in some way.

3. **Bosses** – You work for these people and report to them.

4. **Casual Acquaintances** – People that you say hi to and know their name but you don't necessarily have a close relationship with.

5. **Work Related Acquaintances** – These are service people that come to your office like computer techs or delivery people. They work on the periphery of your company as vendors or as customers. You know them enough to say hi to them. You may not even know their first name or even have formally introduced yourself to them.

Approaching and Calling Close Friends at Work

Approaching close friends at work is very much like approaching your family members. You want to leverage the relationship and credibility that you have with them so that they will just listen to something. We can assume that you have their cell number since you are close friends but if you don't, you can say:

Script # 5

Getting a Close Work Friend's Cell Number

RM: *"Hey Dan, you know as long as I've known you, I don't know what your cell number is. I've got something that I want to call you about outside of work. What's your cell number?"*

Close Work Friend: *"Oh sure, it's 203-768-5689. What do you want to call me about?"*

RM: *"I really don't want to get into that at work because it's not work related. I'll call you tonight or tomorrow night. Is that okay?"*

Close Work Friend: *"Sure Jim, that's fine. Why can't you tell me what you want to talk to me about?"*

RM: *"It's better for you and for me if I don't go into it at work. It can wait. I'll call you in the next night or two."*

Remember, this approach can work because you are close to this person. If you are not close to them, do not just jump right into asking for their cell number. Again, when you are close to someone, you can leverage the relationship and just go ahead and ask them for things without giving them reasons.

Script #6

Making the Call to the Close Work Friend

RM: *"Hi Dan, it's Jim. How ya doing? Good. Listen, Dan, you remember the other day when I asked for your cell number? Good. Well, the reason that I wanted to talk to you is that some friends of mine from _____have a business down there that's growing fast. Even though the economy is down, they're expanding. I think the idea has some great potential. As a personal favor to me, I just need you to listen for a few minutes about the concept because I want you to know what I'm doing and there might be some money making potential for you. What night should I come over for coffee? Is Monday good or is Tuesday night better?"*

Close Work Friend: *"Well sure Jim, I'll listen to you, but what's it all about? Can't you tell me about it over the phone?"*

RM: *"Dan, I'd rather not get into the details on the phone. It's better for you and for me if we just talk about it in person. Is that okay?"*

Close Work Friend: *"Sure Jim, I guess that's okay."*

RM: *"Good. When should I come over? Monday night or Tuesday night?"*

Close Work Friend: *"Well Tuesday is good. But I don't understand why you can't tell me about it right now and give me some idea of what it's about."*

RM: *"Dan, you trust me, don't you?"*

Close Work Friend: *"Sure, I trust you. I'm just very curious about all the secrecy. I thought we were friends."*

RM: *"Well, I'm glad you trust me. Do me this favor, would you? I assume that I have some level of credibility with you. I just need you to listen for 15 minutes; that's all. Can you do that for me?"*

Close Work Friend: *"Sure Jim, I can do that for you. Come over on Tuesday night. I'll put the coffee on."*

Just as in our previous example with family members you are depending on your credibility with the person to open up the door for you. Notice again that you DO NOT have to answer their questions. If they are a close work friend then they should trust you enough to sit down and listen to you about something that is important to you. If they won't even sit down to listen to you then perhaps they are not as good as friend as you thought or you don't have as much credibility with them as you thought.

Note: The good news about sharing the business with close friends is that you can also ask them to keep quiet around work about your involvement in the business. If they decide to come into the business with you, then you can both start to approach your other work friends. If they don't come into the business with you, you can sign them up as a preferred customer and you can ask them to keep your involvement with your business close to their vest.

Making the Call to a Subordinate

Approaching people that work for you can have some advantages and disadvantages. Of course, a main advantage is that they probably look up to you in some way and respect you because you are the owner of the business or their boss. This is good. The disadvantage may be that they may look at you in a different way because you are building another business outside of work. Of course, they can infer from that whatever they want and that is really none of your business. Make sure before you approach people that work for you, YOU don't feel that by sharing the business with them, you will compromise your position of authority with them in any way. If you feel that you will be compromised, then perhaps you might want to pass on sharing your opportunity with them for now. There are many other people within your work environment that you can approach. If you feel this category will hurt you, leave it alone.

Your subordinate may be a close friend of yours. If so, use the previous approach for a close work friend close to verbatim. If they are not a close friend, then your approach will have to change a bit because you really don't have the ability to use the *"trust"* approach so strongly. You would however, use the same approach to get their cell number as in the previous example. Let's assume that you have their cell number and are going to make the call:

Script # 7

Calling Someone Who Works for You

RM: *"Hi Bill, this is Al. How are you? Good. Listen Al, you remember the other day when I asked you for your cell number? Good. The reason that I did that is that you probably don't know this about me but besides my work at the company, I also have a business interest with some friends that have a company out of the _____area that is growing fast. Even though the economy is down, they're expanding. I think the idea has some great potential. I want to sit down with you and explain it to you because I think there is some money making potential there for you as well. If we sat down for 15 or 20 minutes for coffee and went over the details, and I showed you something that didn't fit for you, would you be comfortable giving me your honest opinion and tell me, 'No,' if it wasn't right for you?"*

Subordinate: *"Sure I can tell you 'No,' but what's it all about?"*

RM: *"I'd rather not get into the details over the phone. It would be better for you and for me if we met in person and talked about it. Is it okay if we do it that way?"*

Subordinate: *"I guess so. Sure"*

RM: *"Great. What day should we meet...?"*

Calling Your Superiors

This category may also be tricky because you may not want your bosses to know that you are considering things other than just working for them. Again, if you feel you will be negatively affected in some way, then hold off approaching them for now. If you feel that there will be no negative effects, then go ahead.

Script # 8

Calling Someone That You Work For

RM: *"Hi David, this is Steve. Do you remember the other day when I asked you for your cell number so that I could give you a call outside of work? Well, Dave, you probably don't know this about me but besides being the Manager of Operations at our company, I also have a business interest with some friends that have a company out of the _____ area that is growing fast. Even though the economy is down, they're expanding. I think the idea has some great potential and I want to sit down with you and explain it to you because I think there is some money making potential there for you as well. If we sat down for 15 or 20 minutes for coffee and went over the details, if I showed you something that didn't fit for you, would you be* *comfortable giving me your honest opinion and tell me, 'No' if it wasn't right for you?"*

Boss: *"Sure I can tell you 'No,' but what's it all about..."*

And we're off and running again!

Calling Casual Work Acquaintances

These are people that you might know from other departments in your company or see in the hallway at work. You may only know their names and just say hi to them or are cordial to them because you work for the same company. Because you really don't know them, it would seem somewhat out of place for you to all of a sudden stop them and ask them for their cell number. So, guess what? You've got to get to know them! You might want to start warming them up several weeks or even a month before you approach them. Find a way to stop them and talk with them a little. Something as simple as *"Hey Janet, you know I say hi to you all the time but I don't know exactly what you do here for the company,"* can start more of a relationship with the person. Once you have established a little more of a relationship, you can now use the technique of asking for their cell number to give them a call about something outside of work. The approach for the cell number and the phone call can be exactly the same as the ones you have used before. If you feel that you really don't know them well at all you might want to add an extra nuance to your approach when asking for the phone number:

Getting the Cell Number of a Casual Work Acquaintance

RM: *"Hi Janet. How are you? Good. Hey Janet you probably don't know this about me, but I have a business interest with some very successful friends who have a company that's expanding fast, even though the economy is slow. They've asked me to make some introductions to them of people that I thought had some drive and ambition and were motivated to make money. Does that sound like you?"*

Work Acquaintance: *"Sure, that sounds like me. What is it all about – what would I be doing?"*

RM: *"Now's not the time or the place to get into it while we're both working for someone else. Give me your cell number and I'll call you some evening and we can set up a time to talk. Your cell number is...?"*

You will notice here that the extra nuance is that you are qualifying your prospect a little more by asking them if they have drive, ambition and are motivated to make money. I think it is important to note here that if your prospect gets very defensive or does not respond positively to having drive, ambition or is motivated to make money, you can politely end it right there. You don't have to go any further if you don't like their attitude or response to your question. If they really start giving you a hard time, you can just say, *"Oh, I guess it was a mistake to even bring up the idea to you. I can see you're not interested. Let's just forget the whole thing."* Say this sincerely, not like a smart-aleck and turn, walk away and attract someone else who has more ambition!

Script # 10

Calling a Casual Work Acquaintance After You Get Their Cell Number

RM: *"Hi Janet. This is Nicole. How are you doing? Good. Janet, do you remember the other day when I told you that I have some successful friends that are expanding their business? Good. Well, the reason for my call is that I want to find a time when you and I could sit down with you for about 30 minutes, maybe over a cup of coffee. I can show you how the company is expanding, what they're looking for and how we might work together. However, if I showed you something that didn't fit or make sense for you, would you be comfortable giving me your honest opinion and telling me it wasn't a good fit? Could you tell me, "No?"*

Work Acquaintance: *"Sure I can tell you "No."*

RM: *"Good. Now, I'm looking at my calendar. Would sometime right after work be good or would an evening be better to get together?"*

Work Acquaintance: *"I guess we could meet tomorrow after work at the Starbucks right down the street from the office, say at 5:30pm?"*

RM: *"That sounds good. I'll see you then."*

Calling Work Related Acquaintances

These are people that you see or run into around work in many varied capacities. These are people that you come into contact with directly or indirectly as you go about your daily work life. They could be service people that come into your building or they could be receptionists that you meet when you call on a customer. Start training yourself to see these people as prospects who may be interested in your products, your services or in need of an opportunity to make more money. This category of person is a little different because you probably don't do more than give a polite smile or nod to these people. In most cases, you have never been formally introduced and probably don't even know their names. So, you will have to learn how to meet them. Again, if you see them all the time, you want to start the introduction and build a little bit of a relationship with them before you ask for their cell number. It's as simple as this, *"By the way, I see you here all the time when I come to call on Bill and I've never introduced myself. I'm Mike. And you are?" (she responds and you say) "Hi Lynn, it's nice to meet you."* Now, every time you see them in the next month or so, you say hi to them (you must remember their name!) and eventually you'll be able to stop them and ask for their cell phone number. This approach can be exactly as you used in the previous example:

Script # 11

Getting the Cell Number of a Work Related Acquaintance

RM: *"Hi Lynn. How are you? Good. Hey Lynn, you probably don't know this about me but I have a business interest with some friends who have a company that's expanding fast even though the economy is slow. They've asked me to make some introductions to them of people that I thought had some drive and ambition and were motivated to make money. Does that sound like you?"*

Work Related Acquaintance – *"Sure, that sounds like me. I'm always looking for ways to make more money. What's it all about – what would I be doing?"*

RM: *"Now's not the time or the place to get into it while we're both working for someone else. Give me your cell number and I'll call you some evening and we can set up a time to talk. Your cell number is...?"*

Notice the difference in the approach to people that you know casually, have just met or hardly know at all, compared to the people that you know well. You are explaining a bit more and giving them a reason why you approached them. This is a subtle but a monumental difference. When approaching people that you know well, you are simply assuming that they trust you enough to listen. When approaching people that you don't know, the *"trust"* approach doesn't really fly because they don't know you and they have no reason to trust you! So, you have to give them a plausible reason for approaching them or talking to them out of the blue, or it will seem weird to them and will cause them to put their defenses up a little. Telling them that you are looking to make introductions for your business friends and asking them if they are people that have drive, ambition and are money motivated, gives the reason and is a nice qualifying move.

Script # 12

Calling a Work Related Acquaintance After You Get Their Cell Number

RM: *"Hi Lynn. This is Mike. How are you doing? Good. Lynn, do you remember the other day when I told you that I have some successful friends that are expanding their business? Good. Well, the reason for my call is that I want to find a time when you and I could sit down with you for about 30 minutes, maybe over a cup of coffee. I can show you how the company is expanding, what* *they're looking for and how we might work together. However, if I showed you something that didn't fit or make sense for you would you be comfortable giving me your honest opinion and telling me it wasn't a good fit? Could you tell me, "No?"*

Work Related Acquaintance: *"Sure I can tell you "No."*

RM: *"Good. Now, I'm looking at my calendar. Would sometime right after work be good or would an evening be better to get together?"*

Work Related Acquaintance: *"I guess we could meet tomorrow after work at the Starbucks right down the street from the office, say at 5:30pm?"*

RM: *"That sounds good. I'll see you then."*

As we discussed in the beginning of this chapter, there are positives and negatives to prospecting for names and numbers at work, but one thing is for sure: you probably come into contact with a lot of potential distributors in the course of your work day. It's up to you to decide what fits for you and what doesn't, as it relates to prospecting at work. If you decide it's a good *"hunting ground,"* then you can have fun approaching people and getting your story in front of everyone you can. Let's move on to the interesting category of people – people that you know but that you haven't talked to in a while.

Chapter 7

Calling Long Lost Friends, Family, Neighbors and Work Acquaintances

There is a whole category of people that you know but have not seen or been in contact with for a while. These calls are interesting because you have lost touch with these people and have not called them in a long time. In some cases, it could be years since you last contacted them. This doesn't mean that they aren't good prospects, it just means that you have to approach them in a way that reduces the possibility of them feeling that you are only calling them because *"you want something from them."* Remember, even though you haven't talked to them in a while it doesn't matter if you still have close rapport with them or not. If they are looking, they will respond to your approach because they are ready to make some changes. The call goes like this:

Script 13

Calling Long Lost Friends, Family, Neighbors and Work Related Acquaintances

RM: *"Hi Lydia, it's Amy Jones from high school."*

Long Lost Friend: *"Oh my gosh! I can't believe it's you. How long has it been? How are you?"*

RM: *"I'm doing great, Lydia. Listen, I want to find out how your life is and how you and Jim are doing but I do have a business reason for my call. Can I get that part of the call out of the way, so that I can really focus on how you are doing? Would that be okay?"*

Long Lost Friend: *"Sure, I guess so."*

RM: *"Great. The reason for my call is that Dan and I have some friends that have a company out of the _____ area that is growing fast. Even though the economy is down, they're expanding. I think the idea has some great potential and I wanted to sit down with you and explain it to you because I think there is some money making potential there for you as well. If we sat down for 15 or 20 minutes for coffee and went over the details, if I showed you something that didn't fit for you would you be comfortable giving me your honest opinion and tell me, 'No' if it wasn't right for you?"*

Long Lost Friend: *"Sure, I can tell you "No.""*

RM: *"Great. What day do you want to meet? Tuesday, 3:00 pm, Starbucks? Great."* Now, how are you and Jim and the kids doing? They must be big!"

So you can see that this approach lessens the possibility that your prospect will feel used if you spend 15 minutes of small talk and then you hit them with, *"What are you doing Tuesday night? I want you to come to a business presentation."* Be direct and honest when approaching people. They'll appreciate it. Now, we'll move on to a huge category of prospects – the people that you do business with as you leave your home every day.

Chapter 8

Approaching and Calling People That You Buy From and People That Come to Your Home

You come into contact with many people during the day as you go about your daily routine. There are people that you do business with outside of your home and also there are people that come directly to your home to sell or service things for you. These categories of prospects are unique, only in the fact that you may know these people, but usually do not know them well enough to invite them to a family party. You may know some of their names and some you may not. For example, you may get a bright hello from the woman behind the deli counter every morning when she hands you your coffee. You might say hello back and even have a little banter with her about the weather and so on. It's possible that you *"know"* each other but you have never formally introduced yourselves to each other. This is always the first step in approaching people that you buy from or new people that you meet for the first time. You must get on a first name basis as quickly as possible.

In the case of the deli counter example, it is as easy as saying to the deli woman, *"By the way I've been coming here for months, but don't know your name. I'm Michael..."* Hopefully, they will say, *"Hi, I'm Sandra; it's nice to finally meet you."* Now that you know the name, DO NOT at this time try to approach them about the business. Walk away and wait a week or two before you make an approach about the business. Keep saying hello and building the relationship and then one day you can say:

Script # 14

Getting the Cell Number of Someone Who You Buy From Outside Your Home

RM: *"By the way Sandra, you would have no way of knowing this about me, but I know some very successful people in the _____ area that have figured out how to tap into the 100 million baby boomers in this country that want to look better and feel better. The business is growing fast and even though the economy is slow, they're expanding. They asked me to be on the lookout for some ambitious people and make some introductions for them. Why don't you write your name and cell number down here on the back of this card? I'll see if I can make an introduction for you."*

As they are writing you can say, *"By the way, they are pretty busy as am I, so I might not call you back right away. If I don't get back to you immediately, can you be patient?"*

Prospect: *"Yes, I can be patient but what's it all about exactly?"*

RM: *(looking at your watch) "I don't have time to get into that now and I've got to run. I'll get back to you when I can."*

You will notice that this approach is not very warm and fuzzy and that is on purpose. There is a noticeable absence of phrases like *"do you trust me"* or *"as a personal favor to me"* You are really out on the rim here of how you know people. As you get further away from the center of the circle of trust, you need to strengthen your posture and be a little more laid back, as if you don't need them. **The definition of posture is: They are trying to sell you on why you should invite them into your business, not you trying to sell them on why they should come into your business.**

Approaching People When You Already Know Their Names

Many of the people that you see on a day to day basis are people you buy from or the ones that come to your home. You know them well enough to know their names. This could be your dry cleaner, the cashier at any local store that you frequent, your mechanic or the maitre d' at your favorite restaurant. The people that come to your house could consist of your oil or gas delivery person, your mailperson, the pest control person, your landscaper, snow plowing person, dog walker, the parcel delivery person and so on. You may not have a deep relationship with them and probably with most of them you don't do much more than say," *Hi John, there's been more ants in the kitchen lately.*" However, you do know their names and they are potential prospects for your new business.

The only difference in the approach with someone whose name you are familiar with is that you don't have to do the *"introduction"* phase by getting to know their name. So let's imagine that you are picking up your dry cleaning from the owner of the business and you've been going there for years and you know that his name is Rocco. After you have paid, taken the dry cleaning off the hook and started out the door, you pause, turn back and say:

Script # 15

Getting the Cell Number From Someone When You Know Their Name

RM: *"Hey Rocco, you probably don't know this about me but I have a business interest with some very successful people in the _____ area that have figured out how to tap into the 100 million baby boomers in this country that want to look better and feel better with a new technology they've developed.*

The business is growing fast and even though the economy is slow, they're expanding. They asked me to be on the lookout for some sharp people and make some introductions for them. Why don't you write your name and cell number down here on the back of this card and I'll see if I can make an introduction for you?"

As they are writing you can say,

RM: *"By the way, they are pretty busy and so am I, so I might not call you back right away. If I don't get back to you immediately, can you be patient?"*

Prospect: *"Yes, I can be patient but what's it all about exactly?"*

RM: *(looking at your watch) I don't have time to get into that now and I've got to run. I'll get back to you when I can and we can talk more."*

You'll notice that we are just collecting the names and cell numbers from people and bringing them home and writing them on the List. We'll discuss more about how to call these people in the next section.

Calling Back the People That You Buy From or That Come Into Your Home

It is important to remember that even though you *"know"* these people because you see them every day when you get your coffee or they come once a month to your house to do the pest control, you don't have a close relationship with them. They are not your friends. If you start to *"schmooze"* them too much or try to move the relationship to a friendlier basis, it will cause them to be suspicious about your motives: one day you're their dry cleaning customer and today you're inviting them to your house for dinner! Too weird! It's better to keep these calls as business calls and not try to become too friendly for the moment. Simply think of these calls as acquaintances that you happen to know and are able to connect them to a great business opportunity. The call sounds like this:

Script # 16

Calling People Back To Set Up Appointments After You Have Approached Them

RM: *"Hi Rocco, this is MJ. Do you have thirty seconds to talk? Great. Rocco, you remember the other day when I was picking up my dry cleaning, I mentioned to you that I knew some successful people in _____ that had a business that was growing fast even though the economy is down? Good. Well the reason for my call is to set up a time when you and I can meet for a half an hour. I can ask you some questions and give you an overview of the business to see if it might make sense to connect you with them. But Rocco, if we met for a half an hour* and I showed you something that didn't fit for you or didn't make sense to you would you be comfortable giving me your honest opinion. Could you tell me 'No' if it wasn't for you?"

Prospect: *"Yes I could tell you "No."*

RM: *"Good. Now, what day should we meet? Would meeting for coffee during the day be good for you or would it be better to meet in the evening after work…?"*

You Have to Get a Lot of Names and Numbers and Make a Lot of Calls

Now that you have the words to say when meeting people and making the calls, there are four things that you need to do:

1. Find ways to access ALL the people that you have previously come into contact with, all the people that you are going to meet in the future and put their names and cell numbers on a List.

2. Find ways to meet new people and be introduced to new people, get their names and numbers and put them on a List.

3. Punch buttons on a phone on a consistent basis and reach these people *"live"* as quickly as you can in the beginning.

4. Get in front of those people as quickly as you can in the first 90 days of your business and tell your story and the company's story with sincerity and passion.

5. Fill your calendar with as many appointments to show the business to as many people as you can. A good rule of thumb would be to look to have at least two appointments per day, 5 days a week for the first 90 days!

Now, we have been assuming that you have been making contacts and calling with such strong posture that your prospect is not challenging you and allowing you to book the appointment with them. However, it is possible that your prospect might throw you a few curves and not go along with your appointment setting so easily! Let's go to the next chapter and give you some advanced moves for the prospect that has some tough questions for you.

Chapter 9

Handling Objections – What to do when your prospect asks you the tough questions

To be successful in your new Relationship-Marketing business, you are going to have to learn how to handle questions from your prospects. The key to answering questions is *"how"* you answer not, *"what"* you answer. When answering a question or an outright objection, delivering your answer in a straightforward confident manner is essential to being able to get the appointment to show your prospect your entire presentation.

The Whole Presentation

I'm sure you have noticed in my approach, that I always recommend that you hold back on giving the details of your opportunity until you are in a position to give a full presentation to your prospect. This is not because I want you to be deceptive or misleading in any way. The fact is that most prospects, when being sold ANYTHING on this planet, have pre-conceived ideas about what they are interested in and what they are not interested in. If you don't believe me, you are welcome to call up twenty people from your warm-market up and say,

"Hi Bill, I am involved with a new company called Apex Health that has a new nutritional supplement that is revolutionizing the way people take supplements. The company is new but this is a ground floor opportunity. They use a Network-Marketing model to get the product to market so you can make some great money by introducing the product to your friends and associates. Also, if you recruit those people and they introduce the product to their friends, you get paid bonuses and commissions. Now, there's no salary, health-benefits or any guarantee that you will be paid for any of the time or money that you put into this business but I think you and Marsha would be awesome at this and you can make a lot of money doing this. What day do you want to get together to talk some more?"

Now, this would be a totally *"honest"* approach. But, how is it going to work? There are a myriad of things and details that your prospect could misconstrue or misinterpret, as well as many things that get left out of this equation. Let's discuss just a few of them:

1. About 70% of all your prospects process information on a visual level. Talking to someone on the phone only

reaches 20% of the population that processes information on an auditory (sound) level. That means that a huge portion of your *"presentation"* or what you said was not even heard. Without a visual demonstration of what you want to explain to your prospect, most people will not even understand what you are saying, never mind be able to get excited about its potential.

2. There are all kinds of assumptions that your friend can make or associations that they may connect to when you say certain words or phrases. Those connections may or may not be positive. Just some examples: When you say *"supplements,"* they may not even know exactly what you mean. They hear *"pills"* when you meant a nutritional *"drink."* They choked on a pill one time when they were ten and they hate pills so they tell you that they are too busy and wouldn't be interested in something like that. Or, you say *"Network-Marketing model"* and they remember 15 years ago a friend of theirs getting involved with Network-Marketing and their friend became a total whack job and wouldn't stop hounding them about their business. So they tell you, *"No thank you I wouldn't be interested in something like that,"* because they are associating YOUR business approach with the approach of their crazy friend.

3. You say *"ground-floor opportunity"* and your prospect took a job with a *"start up"* tech company that failed during the

"*tech bust*" and was out of work for a year. To them the word "*ground floor*" is terrifying so they tell you, "*I'm really super busy right now. Can you send me a PDF that explains it or do you have a web site that I can look at?*" You give them a web site to look at and agree to call them back in a week but they mysteriously never seem to pick up the phone when you call them back!

4. You say, "*Commissions or bonus checks*" and your prospect watched his father struggle financially, trying to make it in straight commission real estate and his father died broke. You are all excited about the idea of a performance-based model, but when your friend hears "*commission*," all they can think of is struggle and heartbreak. So they tell you, "*You know, I have a really great job and I'm investing money for my future so that wouldn't be for me and I don't want to waste your time.*"

5. You say "*introduce*" the product to their friends and they hear "*selling.*" Their impression of salespeople is less than positive. Actually, all they can think of right now is all the salespeople that were pushy with them or lied to them. Basically, they think that salespeople push products that they don't believe in, hound people to buy things that they don't need, in order to make commissions that they don't deserve. So, the last thing in the world your friend would want to do is "*sell.*" So they say, "*I'm not a salesperson like you. You would be great at something that involves selling.*"

These are some of the common prospecting potholes that you can step into when trying to get your friends to look at your new business and they aren't even the most critical ones.

What's Missing is YOU

The main thing that is missing when you try to explain your approach over the phone is the chance to experience YOU! The reason that I want you to get in front of your prospect and tell your whole story, is that I want them to see, hear and feel YOUR experience with the company that you are excited about. I want them to see your eyes, when you talk about how the product or service helped you. I want them to be looking at your body language, when you tell them about the money that you are making or expect to make. I want them to feel and hear the change in your voice, when you talk about what you expect to do and get from your company. I want them to see, hear and feel the energy popping off of you, when you tell them that you are going to change your life and start manifesting all the money, time and happiness that you've always deserved.

Don't sell yourself short by giving incomplete presentations on the phone or over the cubicle. **YOU are the most valuable asset that your business has! Your recommendation, your energy and your credibility with your prospect will say much more to them than your compensation plan will. Take every opportunity to get** yourself in front of your prospect and let them see the whole deal – including YOU!

The Most Common Question

If you are going to do your best to get yourself in front of your prospect, then it will serve you to try to give as few details as possible. As you can see in the previous scripts, the objective is to give enough information to raise some curiosity to get the appointment. Your hope is that you can leverage your credibility or relationship with your prospect so that they will just meet with you to hear and see more. However, when you use this approach, you are going to get a particular question and the question will be some version of, *"What is this about?"* or *"Why don't you tell me more about it now?"*

A New Concept in Selling: Telling the Truth

It is important to remember that I am not saying that you should withhold the truth from any prospect for the sake of getting in front of them. I am simply suggesting that you do not offer up details that are unnecessary at this point and may destroy your chance of getting a full presentation in front of your prospect. One of my early sales mentors used to say: *"Never answer an unasked question."* This strategy has served me very well in selling over the years. However, I have another rule that is the corollary to the first rule and that is: No lying! It is never okay to lie. So, that being said, if someone asks you a direct question, then I think the honest and right thing to do is to answer it with the truth! What a concept!

If your prospect asks you, *"Is this Network-Marketing?"* you say, *"Yes it is. What has been your experience with Network-Marketing?"* If they ask you, *"Is this XYZ company?"* you say, *"Yes it is. What do you know about it?"* You'll notice that I have you ending your answer with a question, so that you can start to get some more information. If you just answer the question and stop, then I guarantee you that your prospect is going to ask you another question and if you answer that one, they are going to ask you another one. If you've ever been in this situation, you start to resemble a prize-fighter stuck in the corner of the ring getting pummeled! It's not that much fun.

The One Asking the Questions is In Control

If you have studied selling at all, you may heard the concept of answering a question with a question. The art of answering a question with a question is an advanced technique. You should be careful using this technique because it can come off as harsh to your prospect. If it isn't done properly, your prospect may also get the distinct impression that you are avoiding their question and that you are hiding something. That's why I always teach people new to selling to give an answer and then ask a question. This way, the prospect gets their answer and they feel satisfied. However, the second that you give them the answer, you must ask them another question or give them a directive about what you want them to do. If you don't, they will be in control asking the questions. You will get off the phone or walk away with NO appointment. And that's bad for them and it's bad for you! You didn't get a chance to offer them your great opportunity and they didn't get a chance to see the whole picture. You both got cheated!

Don't Cause the Question to Come Up

One of the reasons that the questions, *"What is it?"* or *"What is it all about?"* come up so frequently is that most Relationship-Marketers tend to be too vague and try not to say ANYTHING about what it is. Now, I can assure you that if you want to get a lot of strong, *"What is it?"* questions, just try an approach like: *"Hi John. I know we've been best friends for twenty years. I want to meet you for coffee and show you something that changed my life."* Now, what is your best friend John going to ask you? That's right. He's going to say, *"Sure, what is this thing that changed your life? I'm very curious. What is it?"* Asking your warm-market prospects to meet with you, without telling them why you want to meet with them, is a sure way to get pummeled with questions.

You will notice in the previous scripts that I gave you verbiage that gives your prospects a general idea of what you want to speak to them about without giving them too many details. You want to give them something! In fact, you want to give them little pieces at a time. Then, keep asking for the appointment each time you give them something. So you'll remember from the scripts in chapter 4 that I had you leading with statements like:

"I have some friends in Chicago that started a business that is growing fast, even though the economy is down and they are expanding..." or

"I know some successful people that have figured out how to tap into the 100 million baby boomers that want to look better and feel better"

These phrases give a brief description without giving much of anything. That's the key! Don't avoid giving a description. Give a description but just don't give one that gives too many details. Giving a brief description about what your business is or what market it addresses, gives your prospect the impression that they know what the business is. This is good because if they think they know what it is then they will not ask you, *"What is it?"* Your description should briefly tell what your business is without telling too much about what it really is. You will notice that with these statements you are alluding to the potential of the market; *"100 million baby boomers"* or the potential benefits of the product or the service; *"they want to look better and feel better"* without explaining what the product or the business actually is. This makes your prospect feel like they have some information that makes sense to them. That makes them satisfied that they know enough so they feel comfortable in giving you their cell number or booking an appointment with you.

Here are just a few examples that you can use to explain up front, what your business is. These phrases use the *"boomer"* approach, but you can start by calling the market whatever you want.

I know some successful people that have figured out how to tap into the...

"...100 million baby boomers in this country who want to look better and feel better"

"...100 million baby boomers in this country who want to save money and get out of debt"

"...100 million baby boomers who want to lose weight and have more energy"

"...100 million baby boomers who want to look younger and delay the aging process"

"...100 million baby boomers who want to restructure their mortgage and get out of an adjustable or negative amortization loan"

"...100 million baby boomers that want to save money on... (you name it: telecommunications, insurance,

natural vitamin supplements, electronics, appliances, and so on)

The preceding lines are just some examples you can play around with while you are crafting your description of your business. I would suggest that you ask your sponsor or mentor in the business what they say when they describe their business to a prospect. They have dealt with this approach and have been asked the question, *"What is it?"* over a thousand times already. I guarantee that they have an answer! And I bet, it's a good one. Learn it and practice so that when you describe your business to a prospect or you are answering the question, *"What is it?"* that you could look them right in the eye and deliver it confidently.

Now, if you have already given them a general description of the business and confidently asked them for an appointment, it is still possible that they are going to ask for more information before meeting with you. This is certainly the prospect's right, but you also have rights here! You don't have to answer any more than YOU want to at this point. And like I described before, if you get into the cycle of answering their questions one after another, they take control of YOUR phone call and invite – and we're not going to let that happen, are we?

Answer, Roll and Close

The key to handling objections is to use a technique I call *"Answer, Roll and Close."* When your prospect gives you an objection or asks you a tough question, use the following three step process:

1. **Answer** – Give some kind of answer if you want or make a statement about why you can't or won't answer. You must give them something and it does NOT have to be a good or complete answer. You just need to temporarily satisfy your prospect with something.

2. **Roll** – The second you make your statement, (give your answer) you need to roll into some version of *"but"* or *"however"* immediately. Do not give your prospect a chance to ask follow up questions. This is not a Washington press conference – it's a call to book an appointment!

3. **Close** – The purpose of your call is to get in front of your prospect to tell them your story – the whole story. After you answer and roll, then you *"close"* for the appointment again.

We will assume here that you have already given your generic statement about your business, but the prospect doesn't accept that and asks a follow up question. It looks and sounds like this:

Prospect: *"That's fine Bill, I'll meet with you but what exactly is it? How does the business work? What are you selling?"*

(By the way, this is nice move on the prospect's part telling you that they will meet with but you just need to tell them a little bit more. Don't fall for this one!")

RM: *"John, we have a proprietary technology that helps delay the aging process but the phone isn't the best place to go over the details. It would be better for you and for me if we meet in person. Would Wednesday night be a good night to have coffee and talk or would Thursday be better for you?"*

So, you can see here that your answer is *"we have a proprietary technology that delays the aging process but the phone isn't the place to go over the details. It would be better for both you and me if we meet in person."* You then roll into the *"close"* automatically with *"would Wednesday night be a good night to have coffee and talk or would Thursday night be better?"* Do not pause between your *"answer"* and asking for the appointment. *"roll"* into your *"close"* right away.

Plant Your Feet When Handling Objections

The key to handling objections is to stay solid, plant your feet and hang in there a little bit. It is common for a prospect to ask one or two questions. Be ready and willing to give them some kind of answer (it doesn't have to be a good one) and then ask for the appointment again. Remember that the minute you punch the buttons on a phone to make the call you have one objective: to get your version of an appointment or get your products or your opportunity in front of your prospect. By *"Answering, Rolling and Closing"* once or twice you WILL get the appointment.

Handling Objections From Your Warm-Market

Now, in many of the scripts that I gave you in Chapter 4, I gave you the answers to many of the objections you would get from your warm market. Remember that these are people that you know well. You do not have to be very tricky or stand too tough with them. Your hope with people that you know well, is that they trust you enough to meet with you without needing too many details. And even though you know them well, the most common question they will ask you is a version of, *"Why won't you tell me the details about this right now over the phone?"* Of course, they are trying to pressure you with using the closeness of your relationship, so I taught you to use that right back by saying, *"Do you trust me? Do me this favor, would you?"*

When you are answering questions or handling objections from the people that you love or know well, you should be easy going and nurturing. You do not want to push your warm-market too hard. Let's face it – they are your friends. If they are resistant, back off and wait to approach them again at a later date. As I said before, since you are close to these people, you can *"drip"* on them by showing your example to them as you build your business.

Handling Objections From Your Luke-warm Market

Prospects in your Luke-Warm Market are the people that you know casually or new people that you meet along the way. These are the people that we described earlier, as the people you buy from or people that you know casually from organizations that you are involved in. When approaching or calling these people, you cannot play the *"Do you trust me?"* card because you don't have that kind of relationship with them.

Posture is Critical

The good news about dealing with people that you only know casually or that you just met as a lukewarm contact, is that you don't have to worry about ruining a friendship or having them upset with you if they don't like your approach. This allows you, and actually should force you, to have stronger posture when meeting and calling these people. Since you don't have the leverage of a close relationship, you will have to play the *"posture"* card. **My Relationship-Marketing definition of posture is: they are selling you on why you should meet with them, not you selling them on why they should meet with you.** You can learn much more about this concept of posture when booking appointments in my book, *Double Your Contacts*. Posture means that they need you, not that you need them. This means no begging! You have to come across like you have something that they need or want and that if they want access to it, they are going to have to play the appointment game on your terms.

Answers to Questions and Objections

The following questions or objections are common ones that you may encounter as you are continuing to build your business. You may have run into a few of them already and because you had not heard them before, they caused you to hesitate or they completely stumped you as you were trying to book the appointment.

Warning: These answers are meant to be given to people in a gentle and easy going manner. They are NOT meant to be rude or smart aleck answers and they should not be delivered as such. They may appear to be a little abrupt but your tone of voice should be easygoing, not confrontational. As you deliver each answer, you should be confident and say each line as if it is very "matter of fact." You should project that your answer seems to be the most sensible, logical next step. In addition, do not use any of this verbiage if it does not "feel" good to you. If any of these lines don't feel good to you, then don't use them!

Do you have a web site?

Question: *"Do you have a web site that I can look at first?"*

Answer: *"I do have a web site but that's a second step. The first step is getting together. I have some questions for you and then we can see if it makes sense for me to give you the web site address. Do you have your calendar handy? What day would you like to meet for coffee? Would Wednesday or Thursday morning be good?"*

What's this about?

Question: *"What is this all about? Why don't you tell me about it over the phone and then I'll decide if it makes sense to take my time to meet with you."*

Answer: *"I have a policy. I never do that. What I CAN do is meet with you for about 30 minutes for coffee and ask you some questions. If it makes sense for both of us, we can go forward from there. Would an evening be better to get together or are you available during the day?"*

Is this a pyramid?

Question: *"This sounds like one of those pyramids. Is this a pyramid?"*

Answer: *"A pyramid is illegal. You don't think I would be involved in something illegal, do you?"*

Prospect: *"No, I don't think you are the kind of person who would be involved in something illegal."*

RM: *"Good. Then when would be a good time to get together for coffee for 30 minutes to see if we have any mutual interests? Would lunch time work for you or would an evening after work or after dinner be good for you?"*

I'm too busy

Question: *"I'm too busy to meet with you now. Can you call me back in three months?"*

Answer: *"It sounds like I just haven't caught your interest and that you are trying to tell me 'no' in a nice way. Should I just cross you off my list and move on?"*

Prospect: *"Well, no, it's just that I'm very busy. Can you call in 30 days when I won't be so busy?"*

RM: *"I'm happy to call you back in 30 days. But historically, I know when I mention money making potential and someone wants to put off meeting with me, then they're telling me that they're not that interested or have a reason or don't have the drive to make more money. Is that the case here? Is the idea of a business to make more money just not that appealing to you right now?"*

Prospect: *"Well, I guess that's it. Doing something else with my schedule, even if there's money involved, isn't a priority right now."*

RM: *"That's fine. I appreciate your directness. Call me sometime if that ever changes for you."*

Send me literature first

Question: *"Can you send me some literature on what it's about so I can evaluate it first?"*

Answer: *"Not really. I don't work like that. Let me tell you how I work. What we would need to do is get together for coffee for about 30 minutes and we can ask and answer each other's questions. And of course, if you don't think this is a good fit for you, you could tell me 'No' couldn't you?"*

I'm too busy to meet with you

Question: *"I'm very, very busy and I'm in the middle of XYZ project right now. I don't even have time to see my family at the end of the day. I don't have time to meet or even think about this now. Can you call me back next month?"*

Answer: *"I understand you're busy. My schedule is just as busy, if not busier than yours. I know, for myself, that I would only take a half an hour out of my schedule to look at something that really intrigued me and I thought had some good money* making potential. It sounds like you're not that intrigued. Should we just forget the whole thing and I'll move on to someone else?"

I make enough money already

Question: *"I'm very happy with my career and the money that I make. I'm open to other options to make money, like real estate investments or stocks, but if I have to put any of my personal time in, I'm probably not interested. Would I be required to put any of my personal time into this?"*

Answer: *"Well, _____ as you know, even the most passive of investments require some personal time and attention, even if it's just monitoring the project. I guess the real question here is: would it warrant us sitting down for half an hour to even see if we should go to a next step? Could you invest half an hour to listen to a new idea? Great. What would be a good day to meet for lunch? Is Tuesday good or would Thursday be good?"*

I know someone who lost money in something like this

Question: *"I know someone who lost a lot of money in one of these multi-level schemes. Is this like one of those things?"*

Answer: *"I can't speak to what anyone else has done. If you and I met for a cup of coffee at Starbucks, do you think you'd have* the capacity or the instincts to determine the quality of my character?"

Prospect: *"Sure"*

RM: *"Well, I have the instincts to determine the quality of your character. Is it fair to say if we both feel comfortable, we could go to the next step and if we don't feel comfortable with each other that we won't meet again?"*

Prospect: *"That's fair"*

RM: *"Good. Do you have your calendar handy?"*

Is there selling involved?

Question: *"Is there selling involved?"*

Answer: *"Well, of course, there is. All of us sell our ideas to everyone all day long in everything we do. Now, if we got together for a half an hour over coffee..."*

Do you have to bother your friends?

Question: "Is this one of those things where you have to bother your friends and people you work with?"

Answer: "Well, I would never describe recommending anything that I had conviction and belief in as "bothering someone," but if we met for a half an hour..."

Is this _____(your actual company name)?

Question: *"Is this _____?"*

Answer: *"Yes it is_____. What do you know about it?"*

Is this Network Marketing?

Question: *"Is this Network Marketing?"*

Answer: *"Of course, it is. Traditional companies are cutting back salaries, health benefits and retirement programs. Now if we got together ...."*

Question: *"Is this Network Marketing?"*

Answer: *"Of course, it is. In this economy, the Network-Marketing industry is one of the few that's growing. Can I ask you a question? If we got together and I showed you something that didn't fit or didn't make sense to you, would be comfortable giving me your honest opinion and telling me, "No?"*

What is the product? What does the company do?

Question: *"What is the product? What exactly does the company do?"*

Answer: *"The way that I typically work is that we would need to meet face to face for about 30 minutes and get into the details. I would need to ask you some questions and of course, you can ask me questions. At that point, we can both decide if it* *makes sense to go further. Now, would a Saturday morning be a good time to have coffee and talk or would an evening right after work be better for you?"*

How come you won't answer my questions and just tell me about it over the phone?

Question: *"Why won't you just answer my questions right now over the phone?"*

Answer: *"I have a policy; I never answer questions on the phone. Let me tell you how I work. I would need to meet with you and ask you some questions, and of course, I want you to feel free to ask me ALL of your questions. Based on your answers and my answers, we can decide together, after 15 minutes, whether we should go to the next step or we should end it. Is that fair?"*

Prospect: *"That's fair."*

RM: *"Good. Do you have your calendar handy? What day can we meet at Starbucks for coffee? Is Monday good or would sometime later in the week be better?"*

I don't like making money off my friends

Question: *"Is this one of those things where you have to make money off your friends."*

Answer: *"Well, I would never say that helping my friends to make money and receiving my fair share for helping them is "using them" in any way. Can I ask you a question?"*

Prospect: *"Sure."*

RM: *"Does your employer make money off you?"*

Prospect: *"Of course. A lot of money actually."*

RM: *"Well, I have (had) an employer who makes (made) a lot of money off me and tells me what to and when to do it. But when I work with my friends and make money off them, I treat them with respect and let them do what they want to do, only if they want to do it. Doesn't that sound better?"*

Prospect: *"It does."*

RM: *"Well,_____. What I would need to do is to meet with you for coffee for about 30 minutes..."*

I'm all set

Question: *"I'm all set"*

Answer: *"When someone says to me that they're 'all set' it means to me that I really haven't caught your interest with the idea of making additional income or freeing up some of your time to make more choices. Can I ask you a question?"*

Prospect: *"Sure"*

RM: *"So, when it comes to the amount of money that you're making, you're happy with it and all the needs and wants that you have for you and your family are satisfied – is that right?"*

Prospect: *"Yes, I'm doing fine."*

RM: *"Great. And when it comes to having the time to do the things you want to do when you want to do them, you have the choice to spend time with your family or vacation for months at a time if you choose?"*

Prospect: *"Yes. My time is my own and I can do what I want, when I want to."*

RM: *"Great. You've obviously created a great life for yourself. And when it comes to security, meaning if you don't or can't go to work for a period of time, your income will continue the way you want it to and your expenses are covered?"*

Prospect: *"Yes. I have the best disability policy that money can buy, so if I can't go to work, I get 60% of my income so I'm all set."*

RM: *"It sounds like you're right. You are all set. It sounds like I'm getting off the phone soon – can I ask you one more question before I go?"*

Prospect: *"Yes. One more."*

RM: *"You probably have friends, neighbors or a family member who is not all set, who could use more money, more time or a* more secure income. Who could you refer me to so that I could send a sample of our products to with your compliments?"

How do you get paid? Do I get issued a 1099? Is this straight commission?

Question: *"How do you get paid? Do I get issued a 1099? Is this straight commission?"*

Answer: *"Can I ask you a question?"*

Prospect: *"Sure."*

RM: *"Some people believe that they should be paid only for performing or producing something and some people believe that you should be paid for just putting their time in. I'm looking for people that are willing to work hard, produce a result and be paid accordingly for their performance. Are you the kind of person who wants to just put the time in or are you willing to be paid for producing?"*

Prospect: *"I'm the kind of person who wants to be paid for producing something."*

RM: *"Great. Then what we need to do is set up a time when we can meet for coffee and ask and answer each other's questions..."*

Be Ready to Answer These Questions if They Come Up

Many times Relationship-Marketers will make the calls hoping to avoid these questions. As they are punching buttons they are crossing their fingers and holding their breath hoping that someone doesn't say, *"What's it all about?"* or *"Is there selling involved?"* As you pick up the phone be ready for anything! This is how you will grow!

Drill for Skill

I would suggest that you sit down with these questions and answers written out on a piece of paper and do a **"Drill for Skill"** exercise. Ask your spouse or partner to read each objection to you and practice reading the answer until you can do it automatically without looking. Once these answers become a part of you and you know the response by heart, you will never fear another question or objection again. Making the calls will be fun because you will know that you are solid and that you can handle anything that they throw at you.

Be sure to ask the person that brought you into the business or some upline leader that you trust what kinds of questions that they have heard and how they handled them. They have the experience to know what the questions are going to be and they probably have specific, tailored answers for those questions.

Now that you have the ability to fill your calendar with appointments, you need to make sure that you maximize each appointment and make it productive. The next chapter is all about how to set up the beginning of that appointment, so that you make money, your prospect gets benefits or money and EVERYONE stays motivated.

Chapter 10

The Art of Following Up –
How to book the most
critical appointment

The most important part of the business after securing the initial appointment is the follow up. The success of your business depends on you being able to get in front of your prospect a second time. This, of course, assumes that you have been in front of them for the first time and that you have done a complete presentation. **It is important to recognize the value of meeting with your prospect for a second time within the first 7 days after presenting to them.** Here are just a few of the benefits or reasons why you want to become strong and proficient at follow up.

If your prospect agrees to a follow up appointment and schedules it in their calendar, then you know that you have a person who has seen something that really interests them. It is the closest version of a *"Yes"* short of someone saying they want to bypass the follow up and just buy your starter pack and get started.

Conversely, someone who will not commit to booking another appointment right there is definitely telling you *"No"* but is afraid to say *"No"* to you. These are the people that say: *"I want to think about it"* or *"Let me look at the literature and then I'll get back to you"* or *"I want to do some of my own research."* **Someone who will not book a follow up appointment is telling you *"No."***

When you have a chance to get back with your prospect within 7 days, you have the ability to start building a solid relationship with them. When they see you again, they are more comfortable with you because they *"know"* you. The more times your prospect meets with you, the more comfortable they get with you. If they are comfortable with you, they start to trust you. **Trust is the cornerstone of building a great relationship with them as their sponsor. If they trust you, they will listen to you. If you can get face to face with your prospect within the next 7 days after presenting, you have a high possibility of enrolling them as an associate, independent consultant, representative, distributor and so on.**

Your Presentation May Take Many Forms

The follow up techniques discussed in this chapter are words that can be delivered before and after your particular presentation step that your company or sponsor recommends. Your presentation can and may take many different forms other than a face-to-face presentation, where you then are trying to book another face-to-face presentation. For simplicity, we will use the example of setting up a face-to-face presentation or a one on one. Here are some of the *"presentation"* steps that you may be encouraged to use by your upline mentor.

1. Have your prospect listen to a recorded call – you listen with them or have them listen by themselves.

2. Call your prospect and then tell them you are conferencing in a third party or call your prospect and tell them that your mentor or business partner is already on the line with you.

3. Have your prospect watch a video with you online while you are on the phone with them.

4. Have your prospect attend a live webinar that you present to them or that your upline presents.

5. Have your prospect join a large conference call where they hear the upline present. This could also include having them look at something online or something that you sent to them like a powerpoint presentation.

6. Sit down face-to-face with your prospect and have them watch a video with you on your laptop or on their own television in their own home or office.

7. Have your prospect attend a group presentation in a home, hotel, office or conference room where the upline, sponsor or mentor does a group presentation.

8. Send a sample to your prospect at a distance, ask them to try the sample and then give you their opinion.

Read Between the Lines

The preceding are most of the forms a *"presentation"* can take in the Relationship-Marketing business. I'm sure there are some that are not listed here or will be invented tomorrow. The point is that you will need to insert these opening lines or figure out how to insert them before or after whatever presentation your sponsor recommends that you give.

The Follow Up Starts Before the Presentation

When your prospect sits down to meet with you face to face, they really don't have any idea about what is going to happen. They are curious and possibly a little suspicious about being sold something or being roped into something. If you set up your presentation properly, then your prospect will know what is expected of them and where this is all going.

You can calm your prospect down and get them a little more open minded if you can give the blueprint of what is going to happen during your meeting – and what is going to happen after the meeting. It sounds like this:

Script # 17

What to Say to a Prospect Before You Start Your "Presentation" Step

RM: *"Thanks for inviting me into your home to sit down and talk with you. I really appreciate it. John and Mary, you might remember when I talked to you on the phone I mentioned that I would have some questions for you and we would see if there was anything that might be a fit for you but that if it wasn't a fit, that I would be comfortable hearing you say 'No' if it was "No?"*

Prospects: *"Yes, we remember that. We can honestly tell you 'No' if we don't like it."*

RM: *"Good. Actually there is no real decision to make tonight because I'm not going to ask you to sign anything or even ask you for any money tonight. The only decision that you need to make tonight is a decision to get our calendars out and decide when we can get back together again and talk some more. Can you make that small decision tonight? Can you decide whether or not you should even invite me back?"*

Prospects: *"Sure, that's an easy one."*

RM: *"Good. So in about 30 minutes at 8:00 o'clock or so I'll ask you if it makes sense for us to get together again. Fair?"*

Prospects: *"That's fair."*

RM: *"Okay. Good. Let's get started..."*

The Presentation

Now, at this point, I am going to defer to your sponsor, upline, leader or mentor in your business. They know what they are doing and they know how to present your products, services, company, opportunity and compensation plan. There is a whole book that I could write about presenting your opportunity, but now is not the time. However, I just want to say this: You do not have to be great at presenting and you will probably not do it as well in the first 90 days as your sponsor can. This is okay! Follow their guidance and learn as much as you can about how to present but always remember this one important point:

You always know a little more about your presentation then your prospect does, so to them it appears that you are a genius!

So, relax when you are presenting. Your prospect doesn't know how much you are missing, forgetting or screwing up! **They don't know that you don't know, so don't let on that you don't know and you'll be fine.** Get guidance from

Your First 90 Days in Network Marketing

your mentor in the business and learn as you go. That being said, let's look at how you can end your presentation so that you can get to the next step in the process.

You Think You Are Finished But You Are Just Getting Started

When you finish your presentation, it is very possible that your prospect will look at you and say, *"This is awesome. I trust you and I've been looking for something like this. Here's my credit card, I want to buy the starter pack and go on auto ship!"* Don't hesitate to sign them up, sit them down, make a Names List with them and start calling their warm-market! I'm not kidding. If they are ready – sign them up!

While I think that you should go into the appointment with the expectation of them being excited and signing up on the spot, the reality is that for most people the decision making process in the *"information age"* might be a bit slower for them. When finishing the presentation, many new Relationship-Marketers will ask their prospect questions like, *"So what do you think?"* or *"How do you like it?"* If you don't get the *"We're excited to sign up; how do we get started?"* response it is possible to hear something like, *"Well it sounds good, but of course we need to think about it."* You may think to yourself, *"Well that makes sense. I had to think about it as well and didn't jump right in so that seems logical."*

These are not bad or illogical thoughts. They are fine. The danger is in what typically happens next! Most Relationship-Marketers at this point will give the prospect some collateral materials; DVD's, CD's, literature, first night introduction packs and so on. They will then try to schedule a follow up time, at which point, the prospect will say, *"Well we're not really sure what we want to do at this point, so let us look over this literature and watch the DVD and we will call you in a couple of days. If we don't call you, you can certainly call us to schedule to get together again."*

When a Yes Really Means No

Now, this all sounds fine, lovely and wonderful and everyone leaves smiling, shaking hands and promising to meet again soon. It's a beautiful moment. You skip to your car thinking, *"I've got one! They seemed really attentive, polite, took all the literature and said we would get together soon. I'm on my way!"* Perhaps you even asked your prospects if Wednesday was a good day to call them back and they agreed! You're on Relationship-Marketing cloud nine!

You have to understand what is happening for many of your prospects at this moment. While you are deciding in your head that you want to see them and you are very sure about that decision, they are also making a decision. Many of them are making a decision and that decision is *"No."* However because your prospects have a need for approval and don't want to hurt your feelings in any way, they will nod and tell you that they are interested and will review your materials. Understand this and get it: while they are smiling at you and promising to get together with you again, they are saying to themselves, *"There is no way in heck that I'm going to do something like this. These kinds of businesses make my skin crawl. I can't believe I fell for this approach and drove all the way to Starbucks to see this. Even if I love this product or try this sample, I could never see myself doing this kind of thing!"* They do not have the guts to say this to you so you have a false impression of where you stand with them.

Voice Mail Hell

So you think you've got a hot one and they have no intention of getting together with you again but you don't know that. You call them back in three days and get their voice mail. You leave a nice positive message. You wait two or three days and they don't call you back. You leave another nice message. They don't call you back. You wait a week and then leave a message that's a bit stronger. You say that you are surprised that they aren't returning your call to book that follow up that they said they would (when they we're smiling at you.) If you do happen to reach them live after a couple of weeks of calling them, they either string you along again, telling you that they are too busy to even look at your stuff or make a decision yet or they tell you that they've thought it over and it's not right for them. If you are still new enough and naïve enough, you believe them when they say they are still thinking about it and that they need more time.

The worst part about this scenario, besides the time that you wasted, is that you start renting space in your head to this prospect. They actually start preventing you from being an efficient prospector because you keep them on a List in your head that says that they are going to get into your business. This *"stalking process"* that you have inadvertently started actually slows you down from putting new prospects on your List, calling new prospects and booking appointments.

Stop the Stalking and Book a Follow Up

Now, if you have set up the presentation properly with the wording that I gave you in the previous script, (no. 17) you are in a position to *"close"* or book a follow up appointment using the following approach.

Script # 18

Booking a Follow Up Meeting After the Presentation

RM: *"Now, John and Mary, you remember when I started that I said that there was only one decision to make tonight and that was just a decision to see if you would invite me back to talk some more?"*

Prospects: *"Yes, we remember."*

RM: *"Good. So, did you see something about the products, or the company or the money potential that caught your interest, even in a small way?"*

Prospects: *"Yes. It looks really interesting and the products sound very unique but, of course, we would need to think about it."*

RM: *"Exactly. That's what you should do. And I'm glad that you could see that the products are different from other products. What I'll do is give you some materials that you can look at and listen to. Let's look at our calendars for a day that you can invite me back and we can talk a little more. Let's see, today's Tuesday. How about this same time next Tuesday?"*

Prospects: *"Yes, that's works for us because we are both home on Tuesday nights."*

RM: *"Okay, so I'm marking it in my Blackberry for Tuesday night, the 17th at 7:00pm. Now, let me show you what we call a first night introductory pack that has some literature, DVD's and CD's in it. You'll love this DVD where the founder of our company..."*

Congratulations! You have accomplished something huge here! If you can get your prospects to schedule a second meeting in their calendar and commit, then you are on your way to making these prospects at least, preferred customers, if not business builders that will build an organization that you both will profit from. Now, of course, it is possible as I described previously, that your prospects may be very excited and start asking questions like *"How do we get started?"* or *"How much is the investment?"* or *"When can we start trying some of the products"* If they do, then answer those questions and don't be afraid to do the follow up right there, sign them up, sell them an initial starter pack and get them going! Don't make them wait for a second meeting if you sense, or they say, they are ready to make a decision now.

What to Do if They Won't Book a Follow Up

The previous scenario was nice and easy – too easy! It is very possible that you may have prospects who say to you that they are interested but that they can't book a second meeting with you to talk some more. **In 95% of all cases, when prospects are giving you ANY excuses about why they can't book a second meeting it means that they are NOT really interested.** Because they don't want to feel uncomfortable telling you "No," they will take your first night introductory pack, tell you that they are interested and then never even return your call. I don't tell you this to be negative, I just want you to be ready for the reality of prospects that won't commit to a next meeting. In some rare cases (like they are leaving for a month in Switzerland the next morning) people have legitimate scheduling issues- but most do not. Here is how you handle a conversation like this:

What to Say When Your Prospect Won't Physically Book Another Appointment With You

RM: *"So when did you want to meet again? Is this time next Tuesday good for you again?"*

Prospects: *"Well, actually it's not. Our schedule is pretty busy over the next few weeks. We don't know when we could meet. Maybe you could call us next week."*

RM: *"Well, I understand that. We're all busy. How about if we find a time when I could just pop over for 15 minutes to review the materials that I'm going to leave with you? Could you find 15 minutes, say over the weekend or at some lunch time during the week?"*

Prospects: *"Like we said. We're really tight the next few weeks with the kids' soccer games and working late. We are really interested but we need some time to talk things over. We can call you after we read and listen to this stuff and we'll get together."*

RM: *"Oh I understand and that makes sense to me. (Note: do this next part very softly and in a very nurturing tone) But what I know, historically, is that any person that I show the business to that won't book a time in their calendar to meet again is basically just being nice to me because they don't want to hurt* *my feelings. What they really want to say is that they're not interested. Is that what you're trying to say to me? Are you trying to be nice to me and say that this really didn't catch your interest? Is it a "No?"*

Prospects: *"Yes. We guess that's what we are saying. We really aren't interested in these types of businesses. It's just not us."*

RM: *"Great. I really appreciate your being honest with me. It saves me a lot of time. I noticed when we talked about the concept of moving toward wellness it seemed to intrigue you. Would you like to talk about trying some products and see if we can increase the level of wellness in your home?"*

Prospects: *"That's sounds great because you know the kids get sick all the time during the winter and I..."*

Now you know where you stand and this is a very good thing! You will not be wasting time with a prospect who would have told you "No" in the first place if you had given them the opportunity to.

Remember, that your goal after showing your presentation is to always book the next meeting with your prospect. And after that meeting, your goal is to book the next meeting.

Now, the next meeting might be to introduce them to your upline, or get them to a house meeting or get them to an evening or weekend function. Always book from one meeting to the next. It is a game plan for success in your business.

Speaking of your upline, let's go to the next chapter and talk about listening to someone who is genuinely interested in your success.

Chapter 11

Listen To Your Sponsor – The wheel has already been invented

Listen to your sponsor. They know more about your new business than you do. If your sponsor, enroller, leader or mentor is brand new, you may need to go up the line to find someone with more experience and time in the business but you can usually find that person fairly quickly. Look for someone who not only speaks confidently about the business but who also has achieved some level of success. Usually you will be able to tell this by what is known as their rank, title or promotion level. Unlike the corporate world, Relationship-Marketing titles or rank are only given for performance. So, for the most part you can trust that the person who has achieved that level knows a lot more than you do!

Sometimes new people come into the business of Relationship-Marketing and think that they know better than the people who have built the company into what it is. They don't and you don't! Perhaps you have had success in another business. Unless you achieved a high level in another Relationship-Marketing business, you should not try to re-invent the wheel in this one. Relationship-Marketing is a unique business. Many of the strategies that work in the standard business world, don't work in the Relationship-Marketing arena and employing them will cost you time and money. The people that have achieved rank in your business know what they are doing. Trust them.

Plug Into the System

Your sponsor or leader in your business will usually suggest that you do certain things first to get started. Do them! If they recommend watching a DVD, listening to an introductory CD or reading some literature right away – do it! Don't let that stuff sit on your desk for two weeks before you *"find the time"* to review it. **Remember that speed is your friend in your new business! And remember that your new team will duplicate everything that you do! So, if you want to make money right away, don't procrastinate when you sponsor *"suggests"* that you do something. Do it!**

Meetings and Conference Calls

There is tremendous power in a group of people who have the same goal and are using the same method to achieve that goal. By yourself, you are limited, but by tapping into the energy and wisdom of the rest of the group or the team, you exponentially increase your own power. Get around the other people in your mentor's or enroller's team as quickly as possible. If they have a conference call or local meeting that you can attend, get to the next available one as quickly as possible. Show up on time, if not early, and be open and enthusiastic. Listen, take notes and learn as much as you can. This is your new career, so take it seriously! If you have brought someone new into the business, you will want to get them plugged in right away to the next available conference call or local meeting. It is critical for you and your new people to start seeing the bigger picture and conference calls, webinars or in-person meetings can provide that view. Seeing or hearing the energy of people that are of a like mind, will give you confidence in the company, your products or services and your leadership. This confidence will be a great help to you in the success of your new business.

Major Functions

Your leader may tell you about an upcoming *"major"* meeting where a large group of people from the company will be gathering to share ideas, tips and motivation. **Attendance at these meetings is critical to your success!** Let me say that again: **Attendance at these meetings is critical to your success!** It will be worth it to travel to these types of functions. They will solidify your belief, give you valuable training information and will help you develop the skills that you need to be successful in your new venture. Sometimes, travel expenses are involved. I would suggest that you look at these expenses as an investment in your business. Every business person knows that in order for their business to grow, they need to invest in it. In the standard business world, it is common to invest in rent, in purchasing vehicles or capital equipment or paying for advertising. These are considered normal operating expenses that must be incurred for the business to run and grow. Investing in traveling to a regional training meeting or national convention that your company or leadership puts on is a normal operating expense of building a Relationship-Marketing business. Of course, you are in business for yourself and may build it any way you choose, but you will be missing a great tool to help you build your business if you pass on these functions.

Books

Your leader may recommend certain reading material. Read it! Success in Relationship-Marketing takes a particular skill set and attitude that is normally not required in a traditional job or career. Most corporate jobs or our educational system, quite frankly, do not prepare people for success in a performance based model like Relationship-Marketing.

Reading the right books will help you in many areas of your business. Building your leadership, listening,

prospecting and selling skills are critical to your success. Developing yourself into a person of strong character will help your own personal recruiting and will also help your entire team to grow. Not only will they emulate your speed, but they will also emulate who you are as a person. Ask yourself this question, *"Do I want the members of my team acting like me?"* Putting positive, character building input into your mind will give you more confidence and a more positive attitude which will attract more people to you. There are many famous and fabulous books that can help you in your new venture. Follow the recommendations of your upline mentors and read as much as you can. One new book a month should be, at least, the minimum.

Compact Discs or Audio Downloads

Books on compact disc or downloads that can be loaded on your ipod are extremely valuable because you can listen to great training and motivational talks while you are driving, walking, exercising and so on. Of course, one of the great benefits of audio recordings is that you can rewind or listen to them over and over again until you retain the information. Start making your unproductive time while driving or cleaning the kitchen productive by listening to the audios that your mentor or enroller recommends. They probably have material from your company that they would suggest and they may also have some outside speakers or trainers that they recommend. Listen, listen and listen some more. There is a whole university of learning available on audios and you can access this university with relative ease. Again, the more positive input that you can enter into your brain, the better. You are certainly not increasing your income or developing a more positive attitude by listening to the latest economic news on your car radio, are you?

Promote to Your Team

Your team members won't know that attending meetings, trainings, reading books and listening to audios are important, if you don't tell them. You have to constantly be reminding your newest members how important it is to plug into your mentor's system. When you promote these things throughout your organization, it solidifies everyone and helps your team to grow, both in new associates and in volume. Stop short of being didactic or demanding that your people follow these guidelines, but make sure that you are mentioning how important these things are to building a business fast. **Fast means money and money means retention.** You don't want to have to rebuild your team every six months; and plugging your people into a steady stream of meetings, trainings, audios and books will lessen the likelihood of that happening. Don't be hesitant about promoting things for your team members that will help them grow and make money. Shout it from the rooftops to them!

Edify Your Leadership

To have success in your new business, it is important to *"build up"* your upline leaders to your team members. Of course, I'm not suggesting that you give respect to leaders that haven't earned it, but if you truly believe in your upline's ability to teach, lead and build the business, then talk about it – and talk about it with enthusiasm! The members of your team will be more likely to come to meetings and will be open and willing to learn, if they are excited to hear from your mentors. If you are speaking positively about them, their success and their knowledge, then your team will be knocking each other over trying to get to the next training or function. And that's good for *them* because the more they learn about the business, the faster they will be able to grow. Fast means money and money means retention!

Always Stay Positive Around Your Team

Your team members will emulate your speed and they will copy your attitude. Whenever you are interacting with the people that you have enrolled into the business, you should maintain a high level of excitement and positive talk about EVERYTHING in your life. Your team members don't need to hear anything negative or gossipy from you about anything in your life. You should refrain from ever saying anything that indicates you are unhappy with or having negative challenges with your business. Challenges happen in business. They happen in all kinds of businesses and they happen in Relationship-Marketing businesses. Shipping issues, mistakes, damaged product and computer errors happen sometimes but you should never share any of your frustration with the people that are on your team that look to you for leadership. As the leader, you need to be *"ROCK"* for your people. If you share negative things with them, it starts to shake their belief and they can't take it. If you are frustrated or negative about something that happened in your business, send it up the line to a leader ABOVE you that can handle it and can counsel you accordingly.

Be Coachable

Even if you have fast growth and start succeeding right away in your new business, you don't know it all and you won't know it all. There will almost always be someone up the line in your organization that has things that you want. I'm not just talking about money! They may also have a great family, respect of the community, an abundant spiritual life, joy, happiness, confidence and an ease of living that you would like to emulate. Be coachable. Search for leaders that have what you want and listen to them. Listen to their audios or travel to hear them speak and meet them. If they have earned your respect, then be open to listening to their advice and counsel. The way to keep your business growing is YOU keep growing. Keep expanding by looking for people that you can copy and learn from. There are tremendous benefits to be had from finding great mentors and they don't all come in the form of money or bonus checks.

Expect the Best of Your Team

Expect the best from your people. I have always found that people will rise to your expectations of them. Trust them! Trust that they will work hard, will put new people on their List and will make the calls. Trust them! Trust that they will do the right things and will take the actions that they need to take to develop themselves into the leaders that you know they can be. Trust them! Trust that they will follow your system of success to the best of their ability. **If you trust your people, they will rise to the level of that trust.**

The Secrets to Success Aren't Secrets in the Relationship-Marketing Business

In most businesses in the *"normal"* marketplace you have to fight to learn what your boss or your competitors know. In Relationship-Marketing, the system is set up to be open to you, to share ALL the *"secrets"* of success with you. They aren't hidden! Your sponsor or mentors want you to succeed because they benefit too! It's a symbiotic system that encourages your upline leaders to keep teaching you how to get better and grow. Take advantage of it. Don't be resistant to it. Allow your mentors to help you. Trust them. They know what they're doing. When you pass them in rank, promotion level and income, then you can listen to someone else!

Chapter 12

Conclusion - A day in the life of a Relationship-Marketing Rock Star

Your New Life – What Should it Look Like?

So, what should your life look like now that you are in your new business? Your antenna is always up! You are always on the lookout for people that have drive, ambition and are motivated to make money. As I said in my book, *Double Your Contacts,* you have a *"prospecting consciousness."* You are adding names and numbers to your List on a daily basis. You are making calls EVERY DAY. On my acclaimed double compact disc set, *Overcoming Objections While Booking Appointments* you'll hear me say that you just need to make 3 to 5 calls minimally, EVERY DAY. Don't allow yourself to go a day without making at least 3 or 5 calls to reach out to someone new about your business. Don't allow yourself to get stale or rusty. Stay in motion by doing at least a little bit every day.

Relationship-Marketing Rock Stars carry their Names List with them at all times! They are constantly looking at the names on the list. They focus on prospecting. They are always looking to add new names to the List. By having the List on their person, dashboard or next to their computer at work, they keep their intention strong to get in front of that next new person. In my most popular CD set, *Double Your Contacts,* I discuss the use and reasons for the List in great detail.

Keep expanding, keep growing. Listen to a Compact Disc or an audio download from your upline or a trainer every day. Keep attracting great prospects that are ready by thinking, acting and speaking positively. Smile at everyone you meet. They need it! Read at least a few pages from a book on success, selling or prospecting every day. Keep your belief in yourself, your business and your associates high! Have fun with meeting new people and getting their names and numbers. Enjoy growing and expanding by punching buttons on a phone and messing with your prospects.

Relationship-Marketing Rock Stars attend functions put on by their upline sponsors and mentors. They show up on time. They sit in the front row. They show their downline and sidelines how excited they are and how much they believe by their example. They are always creating and fostering an environment of success wherever they are, especially when they are around their own people. They make opportunity meetings fun and they make trainings informative, educational and worthwhile.

Relationship-Marketing Rock Stars plant their feet when approaching prospects. Whether you are calling your closest friends or meeting someone brand new, know what you believe and stay true to that belief. Don't let someone's negativity about the industry or your company shake you; you're better and stronger than that! Answer their questions with conviction and belief and get the appointment. Show them your products, services on your terms, not theirs. Book follow up appointments with prospects that see the business for the first time. If they won't book the follow up, be strong enough to call them on it and tell them that you understand that they are saying, *"No."*

Relationship-Marketing Rock Stars know that, *"Speed is their friend."* Get a fast start, get momentum on your side and build it fast. Call everyone on your List and get in front of them as fast as you can. Look to get the names off your List in the next 90 days. Push the throttle down 100% and give it the *"the big smash,"* as the pilots say. If something slows you down along the way, don't be afraid to restart again. You can restart your business at any time and give it a 90 day push at any time in your Relationship-Marketing career.

Why not give your new business four 90 day cycles for a year? Give it all you've got for just one year! Get in front of as many people as you can. At the end of the year, you'll know that you have given your best. If it doesn't work, all you will have lost is some money for samples and literature and some time. If it works, you'll be living the life of a Relationship-Marketing Rock Star, sitting on the beach collecting your checks; a pretty good life for working fast for a year or so. I've trained thousands of people who say that it's worth it. You will too!

Quantity Discounts

To make sure that every new distributor, associate, rep, consultant or independent business owner in your organization gets this book the first night they sign up in your opportunity, call Rick Franklin at our Connecticut office for quantity discounts.

Phone: 860-350-6477 or email at
rfranklin@prospectingcafe.com

www.prospectingcafe.com
"Your daily source for prospecting motivation"

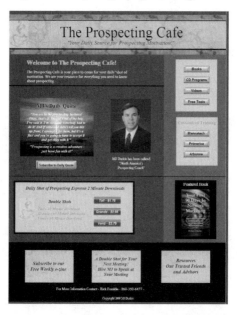

Start your day with a double shot of prospecting espresso! Click on the prospectingcafe.com first thing in the morning to get your absolutely free *"quote of the day"* as well as listen to a new complimentary audio download of MJ Durkin coaching you in the latest breakthrough techniques in prospecting.

Or click in for a leisurely stay in the prospecting cafe. Enjoy a tasty latte, read a book, watch a video or read MJ's blog as he motivates and inspires you to pick up the phone and do the most important part of your job as a salesperson everyday – prospect!

www.prospectingcafe.com It's a great way to start your day!

Double Your Contacts

Published in 2006 this Network-Marketing *"classic"* has sold over 82,000 copies. It is a 35,000 word manual on how to prospect. It covers belief systems, how to add new names to your List if your warm market is gone and has actual scripts with line by line verbiage showing you how to get the appointment to show your opportunity. Go to www.prospectingcafe.com to order yours today. $24.95

Selling from the Heart

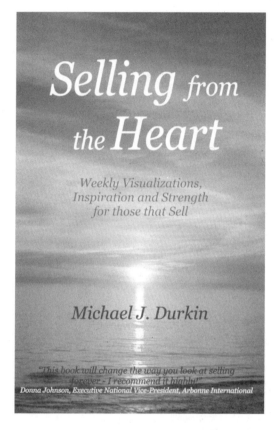

Selling from the Heart is an inspirational and visualization manual for all salespeople. It is set in a 52 week format with a thought, intent and visualization for each week. Selling from the Heart contains concepts to help you create the kind of territory, sales, customers and income that you desire. This book will show you how to have fun again in your sales career! Go to www.prospectingcafe.com to order. $19.95

Double Your Downline

This sequel to Double Your Contacts is for the seasoned Network-Marketer. It contains advanced techniques for booking appointments, securing the follow-up, effectively sending samples and leading your team. This book covers the most common questions of veteran NM's and covers MJ's *"6 Step System"* for prospecting in minute detail. To order go to www.prospectingcafe.com $24.95

Own Your Home Own Your Life

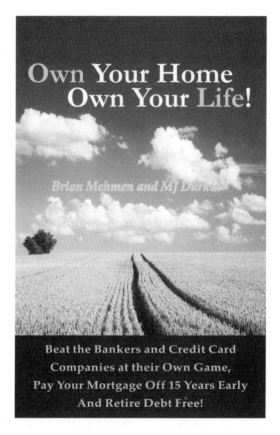

MJ Durkin teams up with financial expert Brian Mehmen to write the manual that America needs to become debt free! Learn how to pay your mortgage off 15 years early, eliminate your credit card debt and save 1.3 million for retirement. This book should be read by every person that has a mortgage and every young person getting ready to enter the home buying market. To order go to www.prospectingcafe.com $15.95

Duplique Sus Contactos

Published in 2006 this Network-Marketing *"classic"* is now available in Spanish. It is a 35,000 word manual on how to prospect. It covers belief systems, how to add new names to your List if your warm market is gone and has actual scripts with line by line verbiage showing you how to get the appointment to show your opportunity. Go to www.prospectingcafe.com to order yours today. $24.95

Doublez Vos Contacts

Published in 2006 this Network-Marketing *"classic"* is now available in French. It is a 35,000 word manual on how to prospect. It covers belief systems, how to add new names to your List if your warm market is gone and has actual scripts with line by line verbiage showing you how to get the appointment to show your opportunity. Go to www.prospectingcafe.com to order yours today. $24.95

About the Author

Selling for twelve years at the kitchen table, MJ Durkin built one of the most profitable and record breaking water treatment dealerships in the country. It was here that he refined his strategies on prospecting. After selling his ten year old service business for $250,000, he started cold calling on corporations and small businesses to build a speaking and sales training business.

In 2005 after successfully training many Fortune 1000 companies, MJ Durkin was approached by several top distributors in a well known Network-Marketing company. Impressed with his emphasis and strong message on prospecting they encouraged him to write a book for their industry. They provided the details about their industry and MJ combined his techniques with Network-Marketing and the book, *Double Your Contacts*, was born. To date, over 82,000 copies of the book have been sold.

MJ Durkin has been a keynote speaker and presenter for some of the world's largest sales organizations. *"North America's Prospecting Coach,"* is known for his irreverent, humorous speaking style, as well as his ability to connect with an audience and keep them engaged.

He is the author of four other books: *Double Your Contacts*: What Every Network Marketer Needs To Know About Contacting and Booking Appointments, *Selling from the Heart:* Weekly Visualizations, Inspiration and Strength for those that Sell, *Own Your Home – Own Your Life:* Beat the Bankers and Credit Card Companies at Their Own Game and Retire Debt Free and *Double Your Downline*: Unlocking the Secrets of Network-Marketing Success.

Double Your Contacts has also been translated into Spanish and French.

MJ Durkin lives in Connecticut with his sons, Corey and Tyler.

If you liked...
"Your First 90 Days In Network Marketing" you'll love MJ Durkin's live training!

Corporate keynote presentations - MJ will rock your next meeting or sales conference with a customized talk for your organization. MJ will invest time with you and your management and leaders, to question you about what your audience needs to hear. Fees for this type of talk start at $10,000 plus expenses.

Network-Marketing Leaders – If your audience is over 250 participants MJ Durkin will waive this fee for an opportunity to market our products. The host invests in a coach plane fare and hotel room.

Power of Belief Seminar – This seminar is ideal if you have a relatively small group of participants that you want to train. This seminar is usually held during the week from 6:30PM till 9:30PM. The fee is $35.00 to $45.00 per participant with a minimum of 70 to 100 participants.

Prospecting Your Way to the KT Seminar - This seminar runs between 4 to 8 hours. It is typically held on a Friday or a Saturday. The fee is $60 to $75.00 per participant with minimums ranging from 70 to 100 people.

Call Rick Franklin for details, availability or to receive a complimentary preview DVD of MJ doing a live training: 860-350-6477 or email him at rfranklin@prospectingcafe.com.